Spectral Realms

No. 15 ‡ Summer 2021

Edited by S. T. Joshi

The spectral realms that thou canst see
With eyes veil'd from the world and me.

H. P. LOVECRAFT, "To a Dreamer"

SPECTRAL REALMS is published twice a year by Hippocampus Press,
P.O. Box 641, New York, NY 10156 (www.hippocampuspress.com).
Copyright © 2021 by Hippocampus Press.
All works are copyright © 2021 by their respective authors.
Cover art and design by Daniel V. Sauer, dansauerdesign.com
Hippocampus Press logo by Anastasia Damianakos.

ISBN 978-1-61498-342-2   ISSN 2333-4215

Contents

Poems

Mother Dearest

Ngo Binh Anh Khoa

Unbridled dread stabs through her heart
As she paces the room
Where not a single curtain's drawn—
A cold abyss of gloom.

The veil of night will quite soon lift,
But he's yet to return,
And with each ticking of the clock
Her mind would faster turn.

The darkest hours have long since passed;
Still, silence greets her ear—
Not one phone call nor message sent;
Within her swells great fear.

"There's still some time before daybreak,"
The lady softly says,
"He will come back. He will. He must!"
Harsh echoes rend the space.

Another, then another hour
So silently flies by
Until just moments close to dawn,
She hears an engine die

And leaps, swift as an arrow loosed
To yank apart the door,
Revealing one tall, pale-skinned form
That she's been waiting for.

With urgency he hides his ride,
A car of black throughout—
Much like a metal coffin which
On four wheels moves about.

Upon his coat and pallid lips
Are traces of blood spilled
With other smells that sicken her,
But she by joy is filled.

Her hands roam over his gaunt frame
To check for injuries,
And so immensely pleased is she
When learning it's not his.

Yet, just as fast as that relief
Has bloomed, it wilts away;
She shoots the teen a glacial glare,
"Why back so late today?"

The boy, exasperated, tired,
Rolls his fierce crimson eyes,
Whose gleam tears through the shadowed room,
And in annoyance sighs.

"Stop fussing, Mom," the boy complains,
"I time my movements well.
There were some meddlers, but they're gone,
As far as I can tell."

She turns the lock and smacks his head;
A snarl distorts her face.
"How can I stop, you reckless whelp!"
Through grinding teeth she says.

"You come back later with each night,
And now it's almost dawn!
Some minutes more and you'd have been
Reduced to ashes—gone!

"Is your game worth so much that you
Would throw your life away?"
She growls. "I shall not tolerate
So foolish a display!

"You're young no more, so act your age
And use your brain to think
On when to move or to retreat;
Don't die over a drink!"

A frigid quietude descends;
They at each other stare
Until the younger one deflates,
Red eyes losing their flare.

"I didn't mean to worry you,"
His silver tongue fails him.
The matriarch waits patiently,
Expression hard and grim.

When she's sure no more words will come,
With one last sigh she'd speak,
"We'll talk more later. Now, you're home,
So go wash up; you reek."

No further argument is made;
As told, the youngster goes
Toward the bathroom for a shower
To spare her delicate nose.

Once he has finished, he sees her
Grab a fur coat and key.
"You have a graveyard shift at work,
So catch some sleep," says she.

The younger being makes to leave,
But he would soon recall
A crucial detail of the date
And say across the hall.

"The full moon shines this very night,"
His eyes upon her land.
"You're gonna be out late?" he asks,
White is his fisted hand.

It's her turn now to roll her eyes,
"Stop fussing for my sake.
I've been at this since times of old;
I know what move to make.

"Though my form's lost, my mind impaired
When that moon vexes me,
The hunger shall not dominate
My rationality."

With one last look toward her ward,
The lady shuts the door
And walks out to the sunlit world
Like countless times before.

She drives her patched-up car to work
At a high school nearby,
One famous for its dropout rate
That's staggeringly high.

From poverty to gangs and crimes,
Problems are everywhere,
So if some were to disappear
Few would sincerely care.

While putting on her janitor clothes
She'd watch as kids stream in;
"I'll bring some takeout home," she speaks
And grins a wolfish grin.

At the evening's close
She ducks out unseen,
Brings a phial of revenge,
Laced the boy's coffee.

Half-asleep, and buzzed
With the celebrations,
He gulps the drink
Down without a thought.

Roars bounce through
Empty rooms, shockwaves
Collide with the silence
Of Midsummer's morning.

He cups his face in both hands;
Paws tangled in a sandy mane.
He almost has his eyes out
With needle-sharp claws.

Four ivory-scythe canines,
A pair of amber splintered eyes,
And an old man's folded flesh,
Mocks from the mirrors' other side.

Epiphany

M. F. Webb

No light resolves beyond the windowpane;
No voice disturbs the silence of the street.
Perhaps a distant foghorn booms refrain,
But from inside the shadow is complete.

Above the trees is one slim glimpse of sky
In which no constellation can be seen,
The foliage a sinister reply
To what by day was bountiful and green.

Where nigh, some vast, primeval god or beast
Is pondering the theft of ancient land
And summoning its vengeance to the feast
With gesture of a broad and tidal hand,

While we poor tiny souls press back the night
With ersatz sun and manufactured light.

October Is Coming

K. A. Opperman

October is coming, as sure as the scythe
Will sweep through the fields of grain.
October is coming, though summer is blithe—
It's just round the bend in the lane.

October is coming, as pumpkins foretell,
Appearing in markets and farms.
October is coming, its mystical spell
Is changing the world with its charms.

October is coming, with cinnamon spice—
With pie and with cider and cake.
October is coming, with treats to entice
Lost children from dreaming to wake.

October is coming, so say your goodbyes
To youth and to yesterday's glow.
The crows are a-circling on blood-colored skies,
And leaves toward oblivion blow.

Plague

Lori R. Lopez

It was going around, spreading willy-nill,
relentlessly catching. Through proximity,
climate, and habitat. In the rain and wind.
  None could be certain how. By magic spell?

A clump of dour Physicians in drab archaic
garb reflecting the somber mood, stark setting,
marched in huddled unison, heads and noses
  curved forth, mimicking a murder-plot of Crows.

Deep rumbles in the background of gray-lidded
skies as the day growled. This brooding flock
anonymously robed and hooded, faces concealed,
  crossed a vacant courtyard under a variety of hats.

Black funereal brims, Corvid beaks, arriving at
double doors half-closed while a torrent spilled.
The bunch disbanded to single-file, unable to
  penetrate the opening (they tried, a clumsy knot).

Led by one, the tallest of the nine, these birds
entered a hall as a river stained red washed
behind: a scarlet stream of mercy-killing
  rinsed off hooked bills and lank oil-cloth coats.

A trail of death. Serious, rigid, the cadre of
Medics regarded each other as best they could,
encased crown to toe in the strange costume
   of Plague Doctors, as if it were the Dark Ages

Or Halloween. It was a time of contagion, a novel
Pandemic. But the age was modern, as every new
year must be. Luther removed a Derby and stated,
   "We did what we could here. All were doomed."

"Cleansing, not curing! The work of soldiers.
We are healers." Calvin, with a narrow Fedora.
Luther stepped toward him. Crimson goggles
   glared. "Do you know of a cure? Then share it!"

Pacing inside a circle, hat in place, words muffled,
Luther intoned: "Isolation faltered. Technology,
advances of Science failed to protect us. Panic,
   paranoia travel with the illness, but we prevail.

Lacking proper equipment, Hazmat Suits in
short supply, a desperate mind gazed to the
Past. It might seem primitive, out-of-date,
   and yet we survive. We are proof we can beat it."

Luther halted right before the smallest form,
who bowed panting. *Unwell.* "Perhaps I have
spoken too soon. Are you okay, Doctor Luce?"
       An intense query. She gave him a thumbs-up.

He persisted. "Let me see." The shake
of a damp Beret-topped head. The Derby
demanded, cutting: "Remove your mask."
       Disobedience. Reluctance. Her gloves rose . . .

To unfasten a snout and still she hesitated,
refusing. After so many hurdles, obstacles
to be admitted and qualify, to keep herself
       unemotional, and for this! A cruel massacre!

Rebecca had feelings. Horrified tears and
anguish flowed. Also doubt and trepidation
gave her pause. What would they do if they
       glimpsed her secret? That she had weakened,

Succumbed. She bore the trademark of
the disease. Though she did not eat eggs
or fowl, any type of meat. Solely plants.
       The malady now passed between humankind . . .

From those infected, some without any
sign. Bec was not as lucky. Revealing
herself must expose a clear symptom!
      Would fellow Empirics have no heart —

And treat her the same as the victims
put out of their misery because they
were changed, impure? Luther reached
      forth to unstrap a dripping ravenesque visor.

And slowly unveiled a revised aspect,
wincing at strange features—Avian,
matching the Mask; the semblance of
      a Rook. Extracting a lengthy blade to slay her . . .

"Behold the Apocalypse!" he raged.
Viewed only as a beast, the female
tore free to cry, "Behold the Future!"
      An echo of brisk footfalls would ring.

Calvin stood for a frozen instant —
wishing the world could return to
a degree of sanity, unity, sympathy.
      Blood wept. A warm heart went cold.

Ballade of the Plague Orgy of Moloch

Wade German

Infection brought His hate and taught us fear;
Miasmal fog has misted every brain
With paranoiac dreams we cannot clear—
Black channel panic, virulent in vein,
Feeds wide-screen imagery of all those slain
Piled high in hecatombs to satisfy
An obese idiot god gone quite insane
Who only wants His worshippers to die.

We bow before Him, humble and austere,
And offer elder souls, that He abstain
From blasting us with dead black eyes that sere.
Beyond all hope the holiest attain,
We pray incessantly with fervent strain,
Accepting that all flesh must mortify
Before the abdication of the reign
Of Him, who wants His worshippers to die.

His temple yawns the void that spawned him here—
The true contagion we cannot contain.
As charnel incense chokes the atmosphere,
With only black oblivion to gain,

We kneel in smoky shadows of His fane
While priests recite a litany of lies.
Above, His idol leers down with disdain
And drooling, wants His worshippers to die.

Prince of the absolute and dark domain,
Can all your wealth forever multiply
With hoard and larder choked with our remains?
Who only wants their worshippers to die?

Télos: The Anxiety of Choice

Maxwell I. Gold

Past obsidian infinities, where crooked spaces and broken dreams were fused together by nuclear cocktails of boiled stars and molten nightmares, I stood at the edge of time. Spheroids of gold and diamonds sparkled in my eyes, as if I could actually touch them, or smell them, or see them. Every single one of them. Billions of pathetically small tetrahedrons, drenched in shades of crimson and blue, floating in the swamps of that black atomic night. I peered into the abyssal maw, the galactic wonders untold painted over my eyes, images surrounded by spiral arms of liquid gas, ice, and rock converging upon a violent entropic storm. It was as if the primal ruins of eternity were somehow seething from the eye of that whirling chaos below.

Inside this geometrically insane equation, I was faced with an insoluble decision, a purposeful delirium as my eyes were glossed over by that amber glint, the anxiety of choice. Above, and to every which way, the possibility of infinity seemed to completely enrapture my pathetic organic consciousness with a liquescent profundity. Below me, however, lay the immensity of time, an ocean of dimensional fluidity where such concepts of the infinite or measured realities were like snowflakes, fragile and useless as they melted away hitting my skin. This was becoming more furious, angrier, as if I was running out of *time*, a choice needed to be made. Ethereal were the last few moments I was able to recall as I stepped forward, past obsidian infinities, where crooked spaces and broken dreams were fused together by nuclear cocktails of boiled stars and molten nightmares, standing at the edge of time.

Close Behind

Frank Coffman

Like one, that on a lonesome road
    Doth walk in fear and dread,
And having once turned round walks on,
    And turns no more his head;
Because he knows, a frightful fiend
    Doth close behind him tread.
      —Coleridge, *The Rime of the Ancient Mariner*

Those flitting forms you think you sometimes see,
Shadows through fog or mist in strange shapes, seeming
To defy all reason—though they appear to be
Close to mankind in mold, like things in dreaming—
Or rather glimpsed in nightmares. But you're awake!
The movement fleeting past "the corner of the eye"
That made you turn and stare—yet nothing's there!
Should not be simply dismissed. For your soul's sake,
Know that these Things have been with Us for aye.
Learn that there are good reasons to beware!

Whether They're "close behind," just out of sight
Beside you, peripheral, just beyond clear vision's ken,
They are the spawn of the darkest kind of Night,
Long banished—They are coming forth again!

The Swamp Maiden

Jordan Zuniga

Lurking in the rivers, nightfall sure to creep,
The sneaking and the mischief with ooze that's sure to seep,
The horrid appearance of an old woman, the melding of her form,
Scent of the murky swamp with treachery to perform.

Village under the moonlight as it plunders an unsuspecting home,
Intent on stealing a precious gem, wherever she may roam,
Her children are the trade-off as she grabs a child from where it lay,
Leaving a monster to wreak havoc wherever it should stay.

The breaking of the dawn and the parents come to find
An image of their pride without a thought in mind,
But gargling would sound in the air, as fear would strike them still,
A monster with rabid teeth and the desire to feed and kill.

The feasting of blood was gruesome on the eastern hemisphere,
Where panic was all but common around the atmosphere,
So the child was taken, as it started to cower,
The demon in the swamp began slowly to devour!

Permian-Triassic

Geoffrey Reiter

They died. The million hosts of species starved
For oxygen in Panthalassa's deep,
Or bodies burning as the magma carved
Its brutal hieroglyphic scarring. Weep
For *Gorgonops*, a corpse dried on the shore,
Dicynodon's deep dying sigh, the blight
Of hot anoxic seas whose poison tore
Into the lonely last dead trilobite.
This was the Dying, vast Earth's gurgling gasp
As red-toothed Nature, careless of the type,
Ensnared all flesh within its ghastly grasp.
But yet, behind a fringe of ferns, a stripe,
Gray-green, a boxy *Lystrosaur*, as day
Dawns new, and once again Life finds a way.

I Awaken in October

Scott J. Couturier

I awaken in October,
just as gaunt ghost-tapers are lit:
I awaken in October as bat
& brume about chimney-hole flit.

I awaken in October
as sheaves shiver in evening's gloam;
I awaken in October as blue
moon's forebear rises, pale as bone.

I awaken in October,
from a September's restless sleep:
scent of decay's succor rises
from heaps of fiery leaves, mounded deep.

I awaken in October,
to a spirit's soft-speaking voice:
fae-folk fret 'mid the clover
as ruddy Jack-o'-Lanterns rejoice.

I awaken in October,
as from some dim-remembered dream—
all shores foreign save this strand
from whence witch-fires lurid gleam.

I awaken in October,
not once or twice, but thrice—
ghosts stalk the waning grain-stubble
docking tails from all the mice.

I awaken in October,
& fear now to sleep again,
lest this far & fair country should
fade, leaving only November's pain.

I awaken in October,
sworn to season's mystic writ—
I awaken in October, ah!
The enchantment & devout Mystery of it.

Reading the Leaves

Ann K. Schwader

No random autumn now. The trees release
their oracles upon the wind for all
October-souled to contemplate. To feed
their dreams toward waking nightmare, written raw
behind their eyes. These lawns leaves drift across
are palimpsests: what ash & cottonwood
wrote yesterday, an afternoon's bright fall
of locust might obliterate. Endure
or not, the message alters. Darkens. Burns
its way along our vision of a time
not yet. Not yet prevented, either. Pull
away, the wind entreats. Retreat inside
until this season spirals to the cold
& merciful oblivion of snow.

What Came of the Search

Steven Withrow

In the catastrophic neighborhoods of Gorham,
    In the rubble of the Saturnine assault,
Where, day sixteen, the searchers from the Forum,
Having found no souls or bodies, called a halt,
    A startled spotter, scraping half a mouse
        From cellar ashes, said,
        Expecting only dead:
There is someone else alive in this old house.

On a wireless set twelve miles away in Hodd
    A uniformed communicant relayed
This message to Sir Favored-More-By-God,
And up the chain of favorites, grade by grade,
    Went word of what the spotter had made clear
        In chatter above his caste
        (Which may have been his last):
The tetrapods left someone living here.

As a consequence of finding the survivor
    The wearied searchers, lessened in their shame,
Were told their quarry was a sand-truck driver
But were not grand enough to learn her name,
    So, when their children asked them for the story
        Of how they fared in Hell,
        They merely could retell:
The lady had no face, and drove a lorry.

The Banquet of Thalassa

Oliver Smith

I heard the loveliest voices call;
ringing in the oaken hull:
sweet as angels, bright as devils,
souls falling in the watery void.
I saw them open time-worn eyes;
crowned in pearls and shells
and unleash death in starlight stolen
from the darkness of a vaster sky.

The ship foundered in the fiery waters
caught in ghostly phosphorescence;
all aflame with older, colder life.
Like the stealthy angler lurking
with her luring-light, she carried me
to cold, black waters where other
beings throbbed and burned like novae
and planets flaming in abyssal night.

Their queen sat enthroned with golden
crown and floating weedy robes
and in her court the ragged corpses
of ages thronged; cadavers clothed
in worm and crab and coral growth—
reef encrusted;
ancients gorged
on the typhoon's drowned remains.

The gluttons feasted in banquets,
centuries long: shades insatiate on flesh.
In palaces grown so deep and built
from fool's-gold and brimstone seeped
from the earth's burnt and bloody wound.
And all around, the boats of ages lay:
among seabed scattered amphora,
precious ox-head ingots piled high.

On the abyssal plain's lifeless mud
the skeletons of sunken galleons rested
crewed by battalions of bones:
brave Jason, Theseus, sly Odysseus,
asleep among bright cities, a thousand
centuries old, rotting in the deep abyss:
their glory gone, their power and purpose
broken now and banished from the sun.

Tremulous Expectancy

Charles Lovecraft

A moment came when winged unbridled thought
Rushed through my soul's mad bent in blinding hail.
Ideas illumed like lights with countless tail
On witching headlands when the sea is fraught.
The drops of stars' bright eyes began to swerve
Out of the depths a glow-worm universe,
Which in my mind instilled a fevered verse
Of magic music filled with soaring verve.
The purple beads of star stairs now reached out
Their soft wild visions that the breath could steal,
While secret pageants of the stellar wheel
Made rolling wonder that soon left no doubt!
I set out boldly from my lightless room
And thought—Would I meet ecstasy or doom?

Assailant from the Unknown

David Barker

As dusk encroached upon the seaport lanes,
I clutched the tome concealed within my coat,
While near me in the surf, a corpse afloat,
Its skull cracked wide showed something ate its brains.
The pier it rubbed was marked with gory stains.
From old brick piles, strange eyes that seemed to gloat
And lusted for the book said to connote
That menace from the stars held men in chains.

The cowled form of a monk lurked on the pier,
And when I passed, he shadowed from behind,
Yet kept his distance to assuage my fear.
This ploy soon failed, for terror seized my mind.
I reached my humble room as stars appeared;
Then through the pane, the weird old monk's face leered!

Inspired by H. P. Lovecraft's sonnet "II. Pursuit" in
Fungi from Yuggoth.

The Call of Lizzie

Carl E. Reed

> The death, then, of a beautiful woman is, unquestionably, the
> most poetical topic in the world.
>
> —Edgar Allan Poe

Part I.

I loved her with a passion
    that would have launched a thousand ships;
her kisses: fire-wine
    that smoldered sweetly on the lips.

We bedded down in fervent need
    in shadowed vale & leafy bower;
innocents no more—ye gods!
    the ecstasy of lost hours

in which we twined our limbs together:
    flexing-rhythmic bucking hips;
frantic, panting, fruited breath
    that perfumed faces as sweat dripped

from golden flesh strung tight & taut.
    We reveled in our youth;
vowed no force would ever part us
    howsoever rough, uncouth.

But Death had other plans—
    as ever with mortal man
our trek through sun-lit lands
    seemed but seconds, then—abyss.

Part II.

Consumption ravaged Lizzie, O!
    how terrible those dark days
that shook her body with ague,
    delirium, chills, malaise.

We married, moved our servants
    to a manse of ivy'd stone;
through gas-lit halls—hand-in-hand—
    we daily whisper-roamed.

How brave her smile; how silken-soft
    those gentle dove-white hands!
Her fevered eyes burned bright and hot:
    I shall return to you again.

Though death take me I know not where
    bliss found is love eternal;
two souls made one shall ever run
    afore powers dark, infernal.

I held her as a last
    harsh, grating, rattling rasp
ripped from her spasming chest.
    She died of the Crimson Cough.

Part III.

Anniversary of Lizzie's death:
    one year from that shattering night
my raven-haired beauty breathed her last
    by cough & candlelight.

I stand in the whited sepulcher
    of her granite mausoleum
heart *thud-thudding* in a cold-clenched chest
    clinging to the shreds of reason

that tell me I am hearing things;
    no lilting alto voice
could have called me from my creaking bed
    terror-thrilled, half-rejoiced.

Beloved has come back to me,
    fought free from the undertow
that threatened to pull her under—
    O! Wherever you go, I go!

Coffin lid hits the floor—
Lizzie rises up once more.
In my ears I hear the roar
of the onrushing ink-black Void.

Black Hymeneal

Manuel Arenas

Azraelle, my moribund bride, gowned in ebon lace,
Down the funest aisle you stride, with exequial pace.
Niveous hands, fingers tipped by sharpened ruby nails:
Little bloodied arrow-tips, which have my heart impaled.
Your fair bosom does not heave, nor stir to respire
Yet enkindles in my core a funereal pyre.
Trailing from your muddy feet, your somber bridal train
Sullied in your brief retreat through boneyards in the rain.
Tangled in its filigree are tokens from the grave.
Upheld by, with impish glee, a grotesque ghoulish knave.
Behind your veil of spider's webs, sable tresses flow.
In rivulets fine and inky, ebb from your dark brow.
Peeling back gossamer mesh, your eyes aglow, like gleeds,
Burning into my weak flesh, to my wan heart, which bleeds.
Crimson labia do stretch into a hungry smile.
Enticing me, poor fey wretch, with lewd and baneful wiles.
Eagerly, I give to you my last remaining breath,
As my lips avow "I do" receive your kiss of Death.

In the Small Hours (moon version)

Chad Hensley

a giant round moon
swallows the night sky
pale gargantuan presence pressing downward
bathing the land in ancient monolithic hues,
like footsteps from a colossal race striding the countryside,
their ghosts buried and forgotten beneath crater and dust,
shimmering in space.

The Final Conquest

Ngo Binh Anh Khoa

The Wight-Mare neighed as it dashed through the fields
Where rotten mountains of maimed corpses rose
Round ruins riddled with snapped swords and shields,
Hellfire blazing where it galloped close.
Earth-tethered ghosts wailed where the white beast sped,
And with the Horseman's fearsome scythe they merged,
Whose blade collected grudges from the dead
And from which smothering malice madly surged.
The raging steed and its Pale Rider raced
Through morbid landscapes rivaling those of Hell
Towards the single living soul they faced;
Resoundingly then echoed his death-knell.
The moon-pale scythe within the Horseman's clasp
Clashed with the red sword in the other's grasp.

No word was spoken there; no word was needed,
For their crossed weapons showed their wills at length.
The last existences there fought, unheeded
Of all else, boasting their unfettered strength.

Harsh lightning clawed apart the smoke-stained sky
When their cursed weapons met in thunderous clashes,
Which spread waves of destruction far and nigh
As both fierce warriors traded furious slashes.

One scythe fused with all hatred of the world
And one blade soaked with godly flesh and blood
Collided while crazed specters shrieked and swirled
Above the wasteland where both staunchly stood.
The Rider, horseless now, fought dauntlessly,
Backed by the phantoms pressing down upon
His arm to raise his might, but in turn, he
Grew slightly slower than the half-god spawn.
Valiant though he was, one second late
In parrying, at long last, sealed his fate.

The Horseman's head rolled where he kneeled, defeated,
Whose death erased the ghosts that plagued this plane.
The demigod claimed his scythe and retreated
To his far-flung and treacherous domain.

Now, on the throne dyed in unfading red
Within a castle built from bones and skulls,
An emperor with a pale crown on his head
There solemnly resides and quietly mulls
O'er blood-drenched conquests of his turbulent past,
Which won him his grand seat midst haughty gods,
And how his comrades, who had once amassed
Beneath his flag against the mounting odds,
Turned traitorous. How he made them writhe

Before him, butchered till their breaths would cease.
Now even Death—his final foe, whose scythe
Proved useless—could not grant him his sought peace.
Transcending Life and Death all on his own,
The Nameless King reigns—evermore—alone.

Carcoza

DJ Tyrer

Dream-vision sideslip
Into a peculiar world
Primal, visceral
Strangely sexual
A marionette approaches
Erratically
Bearing a missive
In an outstretched hand
Proclaiming:
"Follow the yellow-brick road
To Carcoza
Where all dreams come true."
Set forth upon that road
Bright yellow in hue
Past fields of poppies
Yellow not red
To the ruined city
Haunted
By a King in tatters
A beggar king
In a yellow robe.
No mask.
No face.
Nothing.
Do not dare.

To peer behind the curtain
Of his tattered robe:
Only madness and death
Can be found there.
The beggar-king
Stalks those ruins
Alone
Unloved
Yet is a king
Whom emperors serve
Far from the dream-space
That is Carcoza
Where Ozymandias
May yet rule.

Mail-Order Bride

Alicia Hilton

$78.99 was a paltry price for love
a demure mate completely devoted
delivered to his doorstep in a box
big enough for a fridge.

The neighbor's beagle yodeled
chased a boy pedaling a trike
too busy enjoying spring to notice
an old man holding a knife.

Behind the garden shed shedding
tears of joy he unveiled his bride
Madonna lovely Madonna he cried
the wind echoed his sighs.

The virgin's lips were cool and stiff
her robe a lovely shade of periwinkle
his arthritic knees creaked as he knelt
kissed her dainty plastic feet.

Years of sun bleached her cheeks
faded the robe but not his devotion
too infirm to kneel at the shrine
he watched rivals court his bride.

Purring tomcats offered mice
squirrels offered acorns a little girl
brought a bouquet of striped tulips
even the beagle dropped a bone.

The old man collapsed amongst
fallen leaves her dainty feet stepped
over his corpse she wept real tears
and chased the boy pedaling the bike.

Plaything

Manuel Pérez-Campos

Nereid, yellow kelp-eyed with hair as virulence-streaked
as a red tide tendrilling to your omphalos and ensorcelled
by sprigs of Aldrovandra: you of the two snake tails,
tourmaline-scaled, which pivot alarmingly as though ready
to pursue discordant wills: you have bit my cheekbone

as I, a disciple of Sappho in silk slip, leaned out a braceleted
arm when you moaned into the pit of my stomach from
my frail neritic boat where I came to vanish, but not like
this: leaving a mole of blood and infecting me, as though
of the lotus of Khemet I had partaken, with the nightmare

of being your lover: you who can touch the Medusa's thunderbolt:
you have plummeted me into your rapidly shifting radiolarian
enormities until I could breathe the chill like you and live outside
the Queen's English, where no anvils are sparked and no churches
built. I am irksome and ephemeral: you are eternal and placid:

a moment spent in coral elsewheres by you is an aeon to me:
and yet for the nonce we are as two fugitive wallops of moonlight:
Nameless One, you must not consider me lightly: the stars have traveled
enormously to effect this cojoining of us: and though there are forces

in you that are hostile to me, I will not seek to sleep in the coils
of the sand-raising Kraaken if you suffer not to abandon me, when
you no longer fancy tying anemones of hyperphagic gyrings throughout
my titillated hair until their tiny shrieks tug it out into a tremulous
aureole, in that chasm you are native to, in a temple to Thalassa.

Death's Kingdom

Jordan Zuniga

Shadows, lurking, deep within the abyss,
Darkness, creeping, lurking through the mists,
The caverns in the darkest depths,
The shadows there to dwell,
Hopeless in its formation,
Deepest pit of hell,
Ground unstable in its formation,
Spirals as desperate fingers in the sky,
The temporary after-portion
Of where the wicked lie,
Those who hunt the needy,
Rob, and steal, and store,
The murderers and the greedy,
The oppressors of the poor,
Death became their shepherd until all was made whole,
Forcing them to pay the final toll,
Lurking in the darkened realms,
Down in the deepest pit,
Not cheated of his profits,
Nor one to be outwit,
His fortress nigh impregnable,
Taking the best portion for his own,
Abandoning the flock to sit upon his throne,
Doors of endless possibilities,
Each speaking a prophecy,

The fear, enhanced anxieties,
Where death would meet his own eventually,
Clenching on the skulls of the dead,
For they had reaped what they had sown,
A being told through tales of dread,
As he sat on a golden throne,
As he pondered his affairs,
And what was done under the morning sun,
He sighed another breath, releasing all his cares,
"It is already . . . begun . . ."

Lepidoptera, My Sweet

D. L. Myers

The fields and hills spread before her were transformed into fantastic
vistas by the fey light of late afternoon, and great clouds of pollen
sparkled and soared in the cooling air. The tall pines that lined the road
hissed and swayed in the swelling breeze, and she zipped her cardigan
against the chill fingers that stroked her skin with each rising gust. Great
shadows swept among the moving branches that pressed against the sky,
and her eyes were drawn again and again into the arching boughs that
danced in the shifting play of light and dark. A mass of starlings
twittered incessantly somewhere above, and a raven croaked in mournful
response. And then, with a sharp suddenness, they fell silent, as a vast
shadow swept across the road, and she stopped in mid-step breathlessly
listening and scanning the treetops for a glimpse of what frightened the
birds into such abrupt silence. No sign of the eagle or turkey vulture she
assumed had cast the shadow met her intent gaze, and though the path
was well known to her, she felt a certain reluctance to continue on.

She noted that the sun now hung low above the misty hills, and, as
she started forward again, she saw that the path before her was
swallowed by a wondrous, prismatic light whose beautiful colors rippled
and danced on the breeze. Transfixed by the myriad shifting spectra,
which moment by moment approached and surrounded her, she did not
at first see the figure standing among the rainbows. Tall and thin
wearing what appeared to be a heavy cloak and some kind of headdress
from which horn-like projections rose, it wavered in and out of focus,
lost in the coruscating light that played over its form in ever-changing
colors. And then, the figure stepped out of that cloud of light.

She wanted to run, but a numbness had flooded her body, and she could not feel anything but a rising elation that was spreading outward from her chest. An involuntary smile parted her lips, and she stepped forward toward the miraculous being that stood before her. Its eyes were many-faceted and sparkled like brilliant blue topazes set in shimmering gray orbits, and they looked upon her with adoration. All at once it swept her into its arms, and then she was spiraling away from the ground in an arcing dance through the darkening sky. Above the Eastern horizon, the moon rose on a silver mist and into its light she sailed with the sound of powdered wings in her ears.

The Meadows of Night

F. J. Bergmann

> Wide are the meadows of night.
> —Walter de la Mare, "The Wanderers"

Wide are the meadows of night,
Deep are the marshes of thought.
I follow a flickering light,
Faint as a firefly caught

In a vial of thick, greenish glass
That formerly held a liqueur
Whose savor would lure any lass
To fantasies wild and impure.

I had tempted her out to a tryst
On the shore beyond meadow and marsh,
Where the rising tide thundered and hissed,
And all of its voices were harsh.

But none were so harsh as my own,
Once I'd had what she'd come there to give.
Her face was as grey as a stone
As she begged, "O my love, let me live!"

The instrument of her demise
Was in what she had dared to consume.
She sank down, never more to arise,
And I abandoned her there to her doom.

But thereafter in hours of dark
I'd wish myself able to pray
For dawn-song of sparrow and lark
And long for the rising of day.

For during black nights of no moon
When the stars are occluded and blurred
I hear a familiar tune,
And my darkness is drawn to its lure.

The song she sang when we first met:
I thought it a nursery rhyme,
But its music won't leave me—and yet
Its lyrics have faded with time.

It seems to me that her sweet throat
Had chanted a muscular curse,
With venom suffusing each note.
Bespelled with a cantrip in verse,

I search for what cannot be bought,
I follow a treacherous wight.
Deep are the marshes of thought,
Wide are the meadows of night.

Termination Shock

Geoffrey Reiter

We sail past Earth, to dust of rust and war,
The world of blood outspread in channels dark
And barren, where in some great ancient age
Flowed fresh blue water streams into small seas,
Before the force of nature stole the sky
To make proud rage its savage sovereign king.

Yet just beyond his realm, we find the king,
The true king staring toward the stars, his war-
Like eye a gloamy red in stormy sky.
He rules the solar system; in the dark,
The grandeur of his cloud-brown crushing seas
Of gas proclaim him ruler of the age.

His feeble father draped in pallid age
Lies bound in iridescent rings, a king
Himself in aeons past, when frothy seas
Shook with the surge of bestial, lordly war,
And bloated from his children's bones, the dark
Cruel titan loafs in mottled yellow sky.

Far farther still, behold primeval sky
Lie mute and impotent in quiet age,
The mage and mystic in the diamond dark,

The frigid father of the slav'ring king,
Now hidden since the frenzied first old war
And stretched across the silent cyan seas.

A leap 'cross night we see the lord of seas,
Ferocious grandson of the slothful sky,
A child and soldier of titanic war,
Yet also cold and blue and wet with age;
With stoic gaze the ice and crystal king
In dwindled rays peers through unfathomed dark.

And what cold chthonic god reigns in that dark?
Though smaller than the lords of vaporous seas,
In his dominion he, th'abysmal king,
Holds sway in that last deathly step—the sky
Of dreaming maculae, who from his age-
Long sleep may rouse in prophesying war . . .

Beyond, the shocking leap into the dark:
At first, the empty warring chaos seas,
Then brilliant sky, the blinding cosmos' age . . .

The Gathering

M. F. Webb

The dusty years have leached the floorboards dry,
Although the walls have half-succumbed to rain
And spiders have adorned the windowpanes
With drapes of lace and desiccated flies.
Where once a splendid residence stood proud,
A shell remains, mere memories and shrouds.

And yet, and yet! Upon the rising moon
That passes full and satiated high
The orchestra begins its stringèd sigh
And satin whispers congregate the room:
A shout, a peal of laughter in the throng,
A shattered glass, an argument, a song.

By morning all is hushed; no one can spy
A dancer lost in orchestral refrains.
Yet something of festivity remains
A glint that draws the glance of passers-by
The brief reflection of a festive crowd—
A dream to clasp and never speak aloud.

The Costume

Lori R. Lopez

It was of stirring consequence to
a mother named Hortense who
commanded a daughter she
decide what on Earth to be . . .

"While nothing groundbreaking
or tremendously quaking,
at least put some thought,
even if it's store-bought!"

"I should like to be a cat!"
is what the girl said to that,
pointing toward a nimble feline
crawling up a trellis vine.

Mother glanced quickly there,
found the pane of glass bare,
then would deductively wring:
It must be an Alice thing!

"And which manner of kitty
might you fancy most pretty?"
Hortense assumed the best
of her darling's request.

Yet it wasn't quite as trite
with a child of the Night
who craved things occult.
Deirdra weirdly did exult . . .

"It needs to be black.
And give fools a heart attack!"
More devil than a saint,
her gaze made people faint.

So Hortense evoked a name
of inglorious sylvan fame.
"We shall visit Opal Drench."
(An involuntary clench.)

"Known for realistic costumes.
We can also shop for brooms."
Down she marched the murky lane
where you'd have to be insane.

And indeed they might've been
while they left a world of men —
striding midst the fog and trees
until they reached a diocese.

Long abandoned by its flock,
a temple carved of timeless rock,
the hall was practically deserted—
rather gothically converted.

"Hello, hello!" An eerie echo.
All they noticed was a Gecko.
Deirdra's mother bent to speak.
"Are you the Pythoness we seek?"

"It depends if you're a quack."
The lizard fled inside a crack.
"This is my unholy store.
Tell me what you're looking for."

A tall and spindly old lady
straightened up a trifle shady.
The impatient Spellseller
claimed to be no Fortuneteller.

"Dare not keep me in suspense!"
bade the crone to Hortense.
"Well, we need a Cat Costume,
and a Number Three Broom."

"I am not a Fast-Food Line!
  Did you say a Porcupine?"
"Cat! A cat!" Deirdra bawled.
  The bellicose Beldam stonewalled.

"I may have conjured a Fruit Bat.
  There's a lovely Muskrat.
  What about a Horned Toad?"
  The girl threatened to explode.

"Why can't I just be a cat!?"
  fumed a swollen-faced brat.
  Grimbling, grumbling a lot.
"Here's the closest I've got."

  Opal muttered a wee curse.
"It doesn't work in reverse.
  Hope you like your grimalkin look."
  Fur and tail overtook . . .

  Whiskers sprouted quite long.
  Deirdra changed in a sprong.
  Metamorphosis-bent,
  her new state permanent.

A masquerade without end
and no need to pretend.
The Costume fit as if bonded!
A deep rumble responded.

It was quite a great cost,
her humanity lost.
A torn mother would weep,
the price being too steep.

Opal gained a Familiar.
Deirdra thought it peculiar,
but curled up on her lap
for a comfortable nap.

A wild gust of animosity,
a stiff whiff of ferocity
swept home poor Hortense,
lacking memory or sense.

Transformed a bit spotty,
her inklings polkadotty,
the picture of forlorn,
she rocked a phantom-child
shorn—by witchery unborn.

Faust Unrepentant

Josh Maybrook

By moonlight I have passed the gates of Dis,
And I have climbed Golgotha's barren hill;
And I have ventured near a vast abyss
From out whose depths strange voices echo still.
Conveyed on dreadful pinions, I have soared,
Ascending to the highest mountain ledge,
Whence I have seen, past regions unexplored,
The nameless things that haunt Earth's utmost edge.
For all this have I sacrificed my soul:
Salvation's hope expired when, ages since,
I scribed my name upon the Devil's scroll,
Swore fealty unto Lucifer as prince;
Yet I would give my soul again, if e'en
To glimpse a tenth of all that I have seen.

Jack Thunder

Adam Bolivar

Jack Thunder let his hammer fly,
    And cracked the very earth,
From which there came a moan, a cry,
    A shriek of giving birth.

It opened up a door to Hell,
    So entered it did he,
The striking of his silver mell
    As good as any key.

Jack journeyed downwards nine long days,
    His hammer's sparks for light,
The narrow passageways a maze,
    A labyrinth of night.

At last Jack met a pallid imp,
    Who did not have a name,
His walking hampered by a limp,
    Because his leg was lame.

"Now follow me," the goblin bade,
    And led Jack underground,
Where far away a spectre made
    A ghastly shrieking sound.

A starveling wretch this hell-thing was,
    And Jack gave him a scone;

The creature held it in his claws,
    Perplexed at pity shown,

Then wolfed it down in one great bite,
    The first he'd had in years,
And though he fought them back with might,
    His eyes filled up with tears.

They reached a gloomy ruined manse,
    Where Mister Fox was lord;
Jack eyed the piles of bones askance,
    A sordid grisly hoard.

The courtly Fox served Jack strange wine,
    Which in the crystal swirled;
Jack searched the crimson for a sign,
    A way to flee this world.

And then he heard a woman's voice,
    The lilting of a song;
Jack knew he did not have a choice,
    To her he would belong.

"I sing for thee, my wayward Jack,
    Who wanders by the moon,
Who treads at night an ancient track;
    For thee I ever croon."

Jack raised up high his silver mell,
    And with it smashed the door,
Behind which lay a room from Hell,
    Described in nurs'ry lore.

A woman in a scarlet cloak
    In chains from wrists was hung,
And when her chains Jack's hammer broke,
    This puppet fell, unstrung.

Jack's fiendish friend led him away,
    The woman in his arms,
Until they reached the light of day,
    Which fleeting life a-warms.

The Balladress returned to life,
    And picked up her guitar
To sing of Jack, his phantom wife,
    While wandering afar.

Not living yet she was not dead,
    A thousand years she trod;
Her tattered cloak was scarlet red,
    A vampiress of Nod.

Of Masks and Monsters

Maxwell I. Gold

On ancient hills of stone, metal, and dread, rainbows bled from the sky, dripping stardust and tears over the ruined world. At the edge of the cliff face, silhouettes painted by dusty palettes of shadow and doom, scratched the twilight as old bones, with faces masked in death, waited to be released from this estranged isolation. Their joints frozen in history, quarantined at some unspeakable moment in time, never to be spoken of again. The wind howled under the guise of a swirling mass of stars, and pounding lights, flooding through the empty streets of the dead city. Great silver forges that once belched molten fire, now laid bare, cold, and helpless against the wind as it welled up inside the mighty furnaces, expelling into the night, crying like an unholy demon that needed to be exercised.

Past withered columns of plastic and powder, beyond that bleeding hill, a scattered glint of amber and neon lights polluted the horizon. Nothing it seemed would ever be the same as the fulfillment of pale and shallow corporate dreams beguiled the ghosts of phantom plutocrats, who haunted those fields of masks and bones, dressed in their silicone gowns moaning in the emptiness of the dreadful night. The towers from the old city glowed with a green translucence, as if those sickly ghosts were hoping to be cured, to be freed from an unbearable existence. Soon, clouds gathered over the hill, pressing against the faded rainbows, when the wind once again kicked up the dust in tantrum; its fowl screech spilling onto the broken roads and shattered sidewalks, followed by fierce claps of thunder and violent flashes of lightning.

The sad wraiths sheltered in their towers as the storm pounded the Earth even harder, where beyond the hill, no stardust or rainbow was visible; merely the black mass of some protoplasmic cloud spilling over the horizon, like a mask. Manic stars flickered abhorrently above in the silent dark, unable to control themselves as a strange malaise took hold, sterile and bleak. It had been centuries since the last Cyber God had visited this pitiful realm, and those who dwelled here wouldn't forget, though the blight descending from heaving mass of storm clouds was different. The air became stale, thick with an unnatural taste of rust and death that caused the deathless things hiding inside the decaying city to scatter with a direness and profundity, so awful and malevolent. Czronth, the living darkness had infected this existence, plastic faces and metal teeth congealed in bone and blood, transuding black bile from sockets of silent eyes; no longer able to gaze on the world as it once was, but as it always would be, under a mask, living in darkness.

Goblin Laughter

Wade German

Bohemian, I often tramped
    Around the country as a lad;
And once, on a summer night, when camped
    In ruins of Neznámý Hrad,
I stumbled on the Devil's lair:
    An old door rotted through with mould
Had crumbled in; behind, a stair
    Led to the hollow earth untold . . .

Why, you ask, would I enter it?
    Perhaps, that sense of what had been;
Of hidden history . . . Well, shit!
    Adventure summoned me within.
So down I went, with torch in hand;
    Down to the dungeon of the keep.
I had to crouch, I couldn't stand;
    The stair was narrow and quite steep.

Submerged in silent depths it sank
    Through ancient, long-forgotten gloom;
Cobweb-infested, cold and dank,
    It bottomed at a vaulted room:
Where piled upon the cobbled floor—
    Midst shadows which had grown as thick
As spirits on black Lethe's shore—
    There stood an awful stand of sticks:

Old bones arranged . . . but *not aright;*—
    Bizarrely *stacked* upon the stones . . .
And while I puzzled on the sight,
    A set of those entangled bones
Untangled, reassembling parts!
    What pitch black magic had bestowed
Its dreadful animating arts?—
    The skeleton's dark sockets glowed!

Was it a nightmare? Did I dream?
    Was I asleep by fireside?
It was no dream; but I *did* scream,
    For now the spectre's jaw dropped wide:
And goblin laughter from the skull
    Poured forth in shrill, staccato shrieks;
The claustrophobic air was full
    Of laughter high as demon peaks!

The skeleton began to dance
    A jig that churned the charnel dust—
Jangling its chains in frantic prance,
    Shivering off the shackling rust!
The awful jester skipped and twirled
    While juggling femurs, ribs, death's heads;
And all around the shadows whirled
    With spectral laughter of the dead!

I screamed! I screamed: "By God's great throne!"
    And so the spectre dropped its toys—
To play a morbid xylophone,
    Rat-a-tat-tat-ing hollowed noise
As laughter, laughter *came from me,*
    Roaring around the dungeon walls
With black, macabre cacophony
    That conjured lurid grave-ward calls:

Grave-ward calls from the grave immense!
    As fearing minds hallucinate
With sight and sound unsound to sense,
    I visioned, as through a worm-raised gate,
The coffined dead . . . who heckled me!
    And all my horror only spawned
More goblin-bred hilarity!
    Beyond, Hell's blackest layers yawned . . .

My ears and eyes bled as I fled
    From out the ruins, down the hill;
Through forest fog and bog I sped,
    Running with strong, Hell-fearing will—
And still behind, that laughter flowed
    In rivers full of evil mirth,
Beneath the grinning moon that glowed . . .
    I swear, by all my soul is worth.

The *Eden* Spills

P. B. Grant

Corrupt and rank, the *Eden* spills
Its cargo of Miltonic fiends.
We drink of it; it drives us mad.
Some choose the razor; some, the pills.

The truth will out—a leak reveals
That this was always on the cards:
The captain knew his ship was crammed
With bottled screams and shady deals.

Amazed to find themselves immune,
The crew escape and swim to shore,
But all the dead and dying wait
With daggers carved from silver spoons.

Oleander and Wolfsbane

Alicia Hilton

Bridal bouquet
her last cup of tea
his duplicity

Black dahlia
a corpse planted
in his garden

Forget-me-not
paranoia
haunts him

Moonflower
a white wolf's howl
awakens her spirit

Resurrection lily
her corpse
transforms

Wolfsbane
paws emerge
from dirt

Angel's trumpet
her howls are as celestial
as her silver fur

Crown of thorns
wolf claws scratch
killer on his porch

Cherry blossoms
his sanity drifts
into madness

Harvest time
the thresher chews
his corpse

Wild lupine
the white wolf
becomes her mate

Beautiful Beast

Claire Smith

At the evening's close
she ducked out unseen,
brought a phial of revenge,
laced the boy's coffee.

Half-asleep, and buzzed
with the celebrations,
he gulped the drink
down without a thought.

Roars bounced through
empty rooms, shockwaves
collided with the silence
of Midsummer's morning.

He cupped his face in both hands;
paws tangled in a sandy mane.
He almost had his eyes out
with needle-sharp claws.

Four ivory-scythe canines,
a pair of amber splintered eyes,
and an old man's folded flesh,
mocked from the mirrors' other side.

La Villa Infestada

(a sequence of Stornello Sonnets)

Frank Coffman

The Last Pages from
The Journal of Montague LeFanu Blackpool

1.
Looking back, I still ask, "How was I to know?"
That villa on the hill had a wondrous view
Of that valley where stretched out the River Po.

It had seemed the perfect place for my retreat—
From This World, yes—but also *Another* that
I'd sought to enter, not knowing what I'd meet!

But I had entered! My God! the horrors met
If one crosses that threshold! And I cannot
Drive them from my mind—though I yearn to forget.

Foolishly, I thought, "Here . . . here I will be free
From fell fiends that from that *Nether Zone* did fly."
I should have known *They'd* have ways to follow me!

Oh yes, there was brief span—a few bright weeks. . . .
But a *Demon*, soon or late, finds what it seeks.

2.

The days were warm, but shade and evenings cool
September was crawling onward toward the fall.
It seemed my plan had worked. But I was a fool.

On the equinox—a wild and stormy night—
It became clear that the cursed *Forbidden Gate*
I had sought to close again had not shut tight.

The spells I had found in that accursed grimoire
Had worked *too well!* They had opened wide *The Door*,
And *Beings* emerged! Some banished long of yore.

I had succeeded by other chants and spells
To send most back to the deepest, blackest Hells.
But soon I learned it matters not where one dwells.

My meddling magic could not be taken back;
Just my living on had left a trail to track!

3.

So I've fled my hoped for refuge on the hill
From my villa to the village church. But still
I know my *Nemesis* follows—always will!

I seek unlikely hope of sanctuary,
Here in this holy place, yet I am wary.
I know no balm can heal *This Sin* I carry.

Father Medici, man of wisdom and grace,
Went up to the villa to exorcise the place.
I cannot forget the look upon his face. . . .

When he returned it was well into the night.
He told me his ministrations had been for naught.
"The Evil in that place is more than cause for fright!

My son, I fear I do not know what to do;
I've never met such Powers that now plague you.

4.
"I will send word to a friend I have in Rome,
The most successful exorcist of our time.
Perhaps he can undo spells from that cursed tome."

. . .

Today we spent in silence and in prayer
In hopes that the *Demon* could not enter here.
Thus, we've done all we can think of to prepare.

But now the black night has come. All light has sped.
Looking out, there are no bright stars overhead. . . .
In the chapel . . . Oh, Dear God! The priest lays dead!

Now I've locked myself into this cellar room,
This dark, dank place befitting the name of "tomb."
So ends my tale it seems—a much deserved doom . . .

It comes!
       Dear Soul, If you read this, understand
Why I chose, at last, a death by my own hand.

The Haunter of College Hill

David Barker

He strides up Benefit and then down Church,
Past old St. John's where rows of headstones lean.
Long after midnight, not a soul is seen;
Odd shadows quiver and then seem to lurch.
Vile lunar beams illuminate the way.
Ecstatic Poe once frequented these lanes,
Cool air upon his neck, a moon that wanes,
Reminding him of she who would dismay.

Alone, this walker wanders till first light.
Few men are brave enough to follow suit.
The thought of things unholy in the gloom
Excite his mind to realms of vivid fright.
Soon echoes of clawed feet in hot pursuit—
Queued up, a crew of corpses portend doom.

Within the Wood

Abigail Wildes

I walk the forest floor in darkest night,
And you should think my belly full of fright;
For when **you** walk within the black
Each rustle, flutter bids you to run back.
You fear each step, each breath unknown
When out your lantern's candle blown
A growl, a howl, a piercing shriek:
Your hair on end and knees turn weak.

You try to warn me caution should;
But I, my dear,
I am the scariest thing within the wood.

A Bottled Dredge

Charles Lovecraft

The dark sky burned with venomed icy cold.
The sepia of lightless murk had spread
Throughout, like beakered iodine of dread
Swirling in insulin of air's wet mould.
There stumbled through dark glass with homeless moan
A one who searched the lea for some soft spot,
A couch of rustled leaves, of fall as not.
The Dark was waiting him upon its throne.

Upon a hedgerow a cold wreath was bound;
A bird weird song eked from the leery den,
And night's fear face had sucked back from the glen.
Upon the dewy morn the corpse was found
With strangest leaves piled on his missing "head."
There slunk back to the murk the thing that fed.

An Old Bone in the Bluebells

Oliver Smith

I live where pale-shelled Romans crawl; snails
like slow fruit rolling among beech boletus
and scarlet fly agarics; mushroom skin
speckled with magic and poison and deceit
to overfill old Merlin with visions
of skulls glowing over the ancient fort's
terraces and hurtling through midnight skies.

The moon is like the unthawed eyes of men
who met death walking in the January woods;
it leaves the shimmer of life iced inside.
I wait in the wild ground beyond the garden:
uncultivated and heady with dog rose
and night-scented catchfly. Gray winged moths
brush the jasmine; black nectar on their tongues.

I walk the coffin-path, carved point to point,
where fireflies burn in green-lanes; oak-rooted;
filled with perfumed honey from the wild hive
of bees, whose ancestors flew from the south
drawn by new blooming as the glaciers' melt
carved through rock; the tide of Jurassic Lias
rises through limestone, clay, and wolf bones.

I sleep where coiled ammonites and urchins
slip from the ruin's fallen blocks; a place
where a retired centurion raised his crops.
Now star-saturated stones are snaked, wormed,
and coiled in the sibilant tree roots;
and the washed-out ghosts of those ancient seas
submerge the marching legion's memory.

Carrot and Stick

(After Kay Ryan)

Steven Withrow

Confusing the parsnip
with the rod
is bad for the horse
that tows the corpse
and worse for God. If
orders for worship
come to the nose
as a tapering root
of vegetable flesh,
sugared, blessed,
but are taken as a
lash to the muzzle
with the crunch of a
cop's truncheon, then
even those saddled
always with a casket
to shuttle the dead
are sure to become
addled. Safer to
praise with one's
head in a basket.

Shuffling Horror

Carl E. Reed

> I like the zombies being us. Zombies are the blue-collar monsters.
>
> —George Romero

Of all the monsters on late-night TV
'twas zombies that most filled my heart with dread;
for in a lurching corpse I could see *me*:
rotted, ravenous, moaning—roaming dead.
Confronted with stark images of decay
a terrible coldness settled in my bones.
Putrefaction: the process cannot be stayed
less frozen or o'er-chemical'd; I groaned
at thought that all my close beloved someones
sometime must succumb to fatigue & pain;
entropy: disordering midnight sun
would rise to shed its darklight once again.
Woe betide all shambling sentient meat!
Here comes stalking death—sound retreat!

To Kiss Death's Shroud

Scott J. Couturier

Too soon your fair loveliness shorn—
cut like unripened fruit, once-hale
face now deathly pale,
no breath rising to animate your breast
or flood vales with piping song & horn.

Buried within one week's infinite time—
your cheeks now waxen, flaxen hair
grayed by grave's despair.
A white shroud draped over your form—
once-warm, & flushed with life sublime.

I stand sentry at your solemn grave—
for two months' time, come wind or rain
or crueler pangs of pining's pain.
Fever flushes me, mottling my skin
with black blotches, such as corpses have.

Perhaps—I could crawl in to inter
myself adjoining you, looking the part,
Death's eager upstart?
Prying aside the covering-stone is no sin—
within, I reel at resinous stench of myrrh.

There you lie, upon your graven bier:
grave linens enshrine your putrid outline,
by brown excretions defined.
I peel back the cloth to behold corruption
where once dwelt Beauty worthy of tears.

I shall not lie with you—I cannot gaze
upon the maze of worms that is your face,
fungus fuzzing funereal lace!
I flee the tomb in mad haste, bearing
your burial-sheet with me in flight crazed.

Now, I look upon it by soft candlelight—
discern your beloved face revealed in stains
left by those putrescent remains.
At length, I fall in love with you anew,
& drape your sheet over our bed at night.

What joy! After three eves of restless sleep
beside your silhouette, the cloth rises a bit—
like yeasts over fires lit.
I see your supernal profile appear
as feculent fluids spread & seep.

Three more nights, & I lie besides
your plump—perhaps too-plump—form,
reclaim'd from the worm.
Yet, I dare not lift the sheet to behold
what takes mold beneath—what it hides!

On the seventh night you stir & groan.
I drape at last my arm lovingly across
your breast—sick of loss,
I press my love-parched lips to yours.
For what, after Death, can we atone?

The fouled sheet stirs beneath my lust,
twines to enfold my ankles & wrists
with a tight grip that insists.
I feel a linen tongue enter my mouth—
taste mildew wroth, tang of rotted dust.

Still closer I cling, unwilling to eschew
even this sickly phantom in your guise:
count me not unwise.
For what bliss is there as I gasp for air,
enveloped forever by my love for you?

Witch's Tit

Manuel Arenas

I have been bidden to show you
Something which you must see.
I've got a witch's tit you know,
Just behind my left knee.
It's still quite warm with life, although
It's sometimes used to wean,
The teething whelps of *roux-garoux*
At nameless rites, obscene.

Our Ghosts Are Going Away

Darrell Schweitzer

Our ghosts are going away,
thinning out the world
until there is no more magic in it.
No more lingering silhouettes on walls,
no fleeting faces in the windows
of haunted houses.
No more haunted houses for that matter,
just old rooms, the smell of dry wood,
creaking sounds that are merely the walls settling,
and shadows that are merely shadows.
Our ghosts are going away,
leaving us with silent graves,
dry bones, dust,
and the all-devouring void,
which inescapably awaits.

In The Court of the Dragon

DJ Tyrer

In the church of St. Barnabé
Vespers were over;
A figure like a priest in robes
Stood silently by the altar
But those robes were yellow
And tattered,
Not those of a priest;
The figure was not quite a man.
Pray for mercy;
But expect none.

Note: The first two lines are taken from the opening
of the story "In the Court of the Dragon" (1895) by
Robert W. Chambers.

An Ungodly Thing

Jordan Zuniga

It was right before the sun set upon the western horizon,
The ocean had yet to swallow the light,
The stars yet to reveal their formation,
While the moon had not yet claimed her portion of time,
And the sky was cold and dismal.

The storm that lingered over the midst of day,
As the clouds became a veil over the heavens.
The wind's touch relayed a shiver by a mere touch.
It was an eerie standstill as no sound was raised upon the open fields.

I remember it, I remember it well.
The quietness all around the atmosphere.
Peaceful, tranquil, serene.

But then, the wind became bitter and fierce as it changed its course,
The raging movement of the trees swayed with unyielding aggression,
And the darkness grew in strength.

Then shadows came, and the darkness claimed its portion.
It crept slowly as I lay incapable of moving,
Paralyzed by fear . . .
Manifesting itself slowly but surely,
As my heart began to pace.
So it slowly appeared for its performance,
As a horrifying bridesmaid denied her heart's desire,

Like a woman furious at the murderer of her husband,
As a terror at the peak hour,
Like a proclamation of horror from the fiercest scream,
She came . . .
Her eyes pitch black, dressed in grey and devoid of hope,
The sound of a deep voice foretelling of despair,
"DOOM! DOOM HAS COME!
DOOM HAS COME AT THE SOUNDING OF THE DRUM!"
As the sunlight arose with my eyes breaking from slumber,
And was released from the nightmare,
So I shivered at the thought of such terrors,
That dwelled in the nightfall . . .

Uses of Enchantment

F. J. Bergmann

My husband is drawing black threads
out of my skull, evanescent, sooty strands
that smudge, smokelike into the invisible air
we always forget to breathe. Nothing sagacious
about this; it's all a fully automated process.

Progress is made: hair-thin passages remain
curled up underneath the reticent surface,
wound around the spindle of the moon. A void
exists beneath mass, into which we are tumbling;
we like to think of it as an inverse zenith.

Something seeps or crawls into the created
crevices, replacing whatever inky murkiness
was lost into the atmosphere. From its substance,
I will release new dissipations to prance lightly
upon lunar leas, then tally results. Manifestly,

lesser manifestations may be summoned at will.
During our next trick, for which an assistant
is required (not necessarily a lovely one),
we will effortlessly debride and unravel
the strangling cords of the heart.

Allure of the Western Sky

Jay Sturner

He wandered by day, wrote poems by firelight,
of dry riverbeds and nuggets' golden glare,
of Native artistry, elf owl wisdom, moonlight
deep in the whiskey of his Mason jar. Drunk as a
dust devil; he and the coyotes all howling—Awoooo!

He wrote of city life left behind—good riddance!—
of art-nature-soul in perfect harmony,
his muses born of red rock and desert sky,
painted horizons bringing him to his knees.

At other times, in the grip of peyote, he wrote
of card-playing scorpions on his sleeping chest,
of snakes much too large, their rattles echoing
through the canyon of his psyche. Nerves prickly as a
cactus; all the upright coyotes dancing, dancing.

In later days he named and spoke to boulders,
wrote pitiful letters to his wife back in the city.
He shuddered now beneath that dark, *ceaseless* sky,
its star-oozing nights too deep, too unknown!

Some say the self-inflicted gunshot stank of fear.
Some say evil spirits. Others, artistic failure.

Some say the West just ain't no place for a poet.

"Shadows, You Say"

Frank Coffman

> Shadows, you say, mirages of the brain!
> I know not, faith, not I.
> Is it more strange the dead should walk again
> That that the quick should die?
> —Thomas Bailey Aldrich, "Apparitions"

It is fitting that they roam the noon of night,
Cool darkness, or amidst stark Winter's chill,
Or ride the gust that suddenly assails
Our cheek made pallid by a sudden fright.
Their life-shells left begraved, but spirits will
Escape bone-cages—and all Reason fails
To make accounting for their stark return.
Especially in places dire, remote,
In deep woods, in old houses where foul crimes still lie.
Most deem them merely "shadows" and they yearn
To find some logic to those things we note—
Watching Things caught in the "corner of the eye."
A myriad number of the numberless dead
Hie hither after the house of flesh is shed.

Surely some are would-be avengers, cruelly slain,
Those doomed to enact their end again and again,
Residual phantoms who plague a place until
Their killers meet the Justice they deserve.
Others—so anger-laden in sinful life—

They return to us by force of evil will.
Only tormenting living souls will serve
Their purpose. And the ghostly ranks are rife
With souls of those who have not yet realized
That they are dead! Trapped, lost in that vast
Beyond, unwilling to accept the life they prized
Is gone. Some, summoned through that *Gate* once passed,
By thoughtless acts or Black Arts back through that *Door*
Are here! But what others might through that *Portal* pour?

Yes, They are with us here and no mere "shadows."
Those moaning winds, the "ghost lights" through the trees,
Those thoughts that something is watching, something follows,
Those semi-articulate whispers on the breeze—
They are not all illusions, tricks of nature,
Some are our oft *unrealized Realities!*
Created beings, no longer within their creature,
But free to share our world just as they please.
The legions of the lost, here left to linger,
In purposed or pained probation in our demesne,
To write upon our world with phantom finger,
That move among us—whether unseen or seen.
Among the mountainous dead there swell huge hosts
Of the disembodied "shadows" we call "ghosts."

Hounds of the Lord

Justin Permenter

A scream echoes throughout the midnight chamber
The song of the strappado and heresies unveiled
Shadows writhe in flickering candlelight
As another sinner's flesh yields its mysteries
    To the iron instruments of God's wrath.

The bailiff bares his vulpine grin
Awaiting his master's command
He counts himself truly blessed
To number among their ranks
    These steadfast hounds of the Lord.

A silent nod compels obedience
The thumbscrew tightens a quarter turn
Secrets gush from a gaping wound
And spill out over the naked stones
    To pool in the cracks between.

The condemned cries out until his lungs burn
His bones crack and splinter with each sickening blow
That falls upon flesh crossed with carmine fissures
Each cut, a tale of sins and blasphemies exposed
    Beneath the wicked kiss of the lash.

At last, his spirit spent, his resistance broken
The prisoner collapses against his fetters
He yields to oblivion's embrace
And bathes in the sweet release of confession
      Before the darkness closes in.

The scribe records each pain-purchased word
A testament wrought in ink as black as blood
"What bliss, what heavenly consolation," he muses,
"To dwell amongst these worthy blackfriars
      These steadfast hounds of the Lord."

The Inquisitor draws beside the insensate body
And extends a single bony hand from within his cassock sleeve
His withered fingers touch the prisoner's bruised and bloodied lips
And trace the dripping edges of the slackened mouth
      As gently as a husband to his bride.

A pang of melancholy washes over him
The disappointment of desires left unfulfilled
His acolytes share in the frustration
Of another penitent soul saved from Hell—
      They would prefer to watch it burn.

The Inquisitor banishes such impious notions
As he ascends the stair to his chamber above
Seeking a well-earned rest from his labors
He knows there will be others to feed the flames
    When the morning dawns.

Soon he and his brothers will assemble in the courtyard
To lift Hosannas by the light of burning heretics
Their song shall ring out above the screams from the pyres
They will sing, *sing*—these instruments of God's vengeance
    These steadfast hounds of the Lord.

A Crow Is Calling

Lori R. Lopez

A Crow is calling, such a desolate sound
Bleak and tuneless—a mournful round
Like chanting or ranting, naming and blaming
Cursing the shadows, a specter of shaming
Offering up plates with Pepper Tarts
Conducting a chorus of Lonely Hearts
For a ravenesque Rook, only one of a feather
Without a Murder, his social tether
Must cry to the night, complexion turned white
Haunting and daunting by dim moonlight.

Laughter out of the Sea

Maxwell I. Gold

I saw a grotesque mass of faces, laughing skulls with broken teeth; compounded together by moist layers of sediment, rock, and regret, climbing from the awful salty depths of the sea. Higher and higher they rose, with corpulent girth and bulk, dripping coarse beads of ocean sweat, cackling and rupturing the sanguinity of my thoughts with a thunderous guffaw. I spied cluttered heaps of clay and flesh smudging the horizon, slopping together abstract shapes and colors as they swallowed the stars themselves. Their laughter was terrifying, infectious and cruel. By nightfall, windows had shattered throughout the city, and buildings sulked in the wake of these silvery iridescent visages, immeasurable in size and dimension, splintering the molten foundations of the Earth.

No one understood or cared to understand the evil rising from the bosom of the planet. Boiling over with callous humor, and wicked hunger, gnashing teeth of smiling masks gnawed at the roots of the world. This insatiable cyberlust, forged in the wild, broken consciousness of humanity's most terrible nightmares, wrought a tattered and wretched plight on the whole of the world. Everyone around me couldn't help but cower, worship even, the phenomena congesting the darkness, towering in multitudinous numbers like a demented pantheon of laughing gods.

My body was aching, convulsing, and twisted in shapes indescribable as my very bones cracked and popped. As I was felled as if by some unnatural cachinnation, a wild music reverberated throughout my misshapen corpse; I'd become an unholy pipe organ blasting out abusive melodies of bedlam. I couldn't stop laughing, even as tears and blood poured from my eyes. My snorting and chuckling spasms grew worse, even as the inconceivable possibilities lurking beyond my future, beyond my face became all too certain. I couldn't help but laugh at the pathetic clay men, whose prayers meant nothing as static and death consumed the salty, bitter night air.

And yet, the faces continued to multiply, growing even larger, birthing more thunderous cackles causing my ears to bleed and burn with an unwilling happiness. Their hollow eye sockets were clogged by a mass of dead squids, mollusks, and other unfortunate creatures; like tears, phosphorescent, miasmic trails of ink, slime, and fungus slammed onto the streets, congealing in heaps of thick sludge that slowly chewed through everything, the city becoming a bloated pile of bubbling ink. Faces, and more faces exploded from the sea with vehement intensity, rising faster, covered in ugly barnacles and foul blooms drenched in brine and poison. Soon, the city had become nothing, the world enamored by laughing faces; swallowing the stars and the sea, and the clay men who foolishly sought to worship them.

Nothing mattered in the laughter of the Cyber Gods, as they rose higher and higher, with corpulent girth and bulk, dripping coarse beads of ocean sweat, cackling with a thunderous guffaw. And the world saw me, a grotesque mass of faces, laughing skulls with broken teeth; compounded together by moist layers of sediment, rock, and regret, climbing out of the awful salty depths of the sea.

Old Sorcery

Wade German

The chronicles of First Age lore have told
Of heinous souls who sought the gates of Hell,
Seeking an evil wisdom each to hold—
Six wizards, each of whom his soul would sell
Without remorse, at demon feet to lay,
If such was named the price he had to pay.
But know: their quest was fraught with jealousy,
Each thinking he himself the best to be;
And each the other held with untold hate,
Until one slew the rest with sorcery
While seeking black beyonds beyond black gates.

And he had bargained: those five souls he sold
To demons, and in this he bartered well
For knowledge of the regions they patrolled,
Of misted mysteries they could dispel:
Of things to offer at Hell's passageway;
Of routes direct, and paths that lead astray;
The arcane syllables of gramarye
To speak in rites of darkest heathenry
So every bend before him would lie straight,
So he would be prepared to wander free
Beyond the black beyond, beyond black gates.

Now north he went, to realms of snow and cold,
And cloistered deep within his citadel

Enclosed by ancient forests, there to dwell
Among the ghosts of overlords of old,
His ancestors to whom he bowed to pray.
He practiced things forbidden, foul and fey,
And he prepared himself by alchemy,
Then voyaged in narcotic reverie
Through astral planes in meditative state,
Where finally he found the silver key
That opens black beyonds beyond black gates.

Arcane the knowledge that he now controlled;
And matter by his mind he could compel.
And so he raised it there: the dark threshold,
Voicing the invocation of his spell:
And darkness darkened, drinking light away
So only purest darkness now held sway;
And looming there, as out some phantasy,
A portal way of night-black ebony:
Beyond, dark gnosis he would consummate
To master worlds, and shape reality
When he returned to earth between black gates.

But know: his path was fated and foretold,
By fate his auguries did not foretell:
The five he sold to Hell had been paroled,

Each revenant let out his dungeon cell;
And howling vengeance that to slake must slay,
Awaited on the threshold of the Way
When he did pass the door, triumphantly:
They dragged him down, each tittering with glee,
To torment, torture, fivefold subjugate
Their enemy for strange eternity
Beyond the black beyond, beyond black gates.

L'ENVOI

Beelzebuul, in that principality
Where every wizard ends in deviltry,
How patiently for all of them you wait,
Weaving your weirding webs of warlockry
Beyond the black beyonds, beyond black gates!

Fatal Attraction

Ngo Binh Anh Khoa

While we were wrestling with the wrathful waves,
My ears were graced with so divine a sound
Above the wailing wind that I turned round
And saw a siren midst these watery graves.
She far outshone all beauties I had seen,
Whose hair, in color, shamed the darkest night
And barely veiled her breast of moonlight-white,
A grace ethereal midst the turbulent scene.

With every rise and ebb in her sweet voice,
More weakened was my fractured self-control
Until a maddening lust consumed me whole;
Against my friends' advice, I made my choice.
In her embrace, I was submerged in bliss,
Swept from the storm unto the calm abyss.

The Damned: A Ghazal

Joshua Gage

With straitjackets and padded cells, we treat diseased and damned.
What cure can quell the frothing lunacies that seize the damned?

Release your soul from bondage. Let it shriek cacophonies.
Give up your body to the Beast that oversees the damned.

A reek of rancid flesh and rot comes wafting through the trees.
We cross ourselves against the stench we fear precedes the damned.

Light the candles. Burn the incense. Scrawl unhallowed runes.
Recite the eldritch benediction to release the damned.

The blade of pure obsidian reflects the waning moon.
A baby's on the altar, an innocent to please the damned.

The Pilgrim wakes the priest and drags him to the sanctuary.
What prayer can be performed? What exorcism frees the damned?

The Bookshop on the Wharf

David Barker

The shop doorbell announced my entry there,
Yet no clerk came to ask what book I sought.
A toad-like creature, black and grim, and squat
Followed me down rows, always in its stare,
But I ignored it, keen on volumes rare,
Yearning after codices left to rot,
As eons pass unmarked, their pages fraught
With evil meant to bring mankind despair.

The worst of these I found in one dark aisle,
A tome hand-writ in script known but to few.
Its rubics penned in red ink that was vile
as blood, graced with designs inspiring grue.
I seized the book, still watched by toadish eyes,
Ran from the shop, amidst a swarm of flies.

Printz's Oratory

Steven Withrow

What drives us to
a private chapel
(far from Lourdes
cathedral) are
words a bishop
shouldn't hear,
not least a
city priest.

Herr Printz,
for instance,
finds it best
to confess
at home, alone,
his gamble with
Azazel in a
pentagram.

Spilled blood
still seems to
keep the demon's
presence, spatters
from a sacrificial
blade—a maid
and trusted butler
shed their essence.

To him, a grimoire
doubles as a bible;
the trouble is
he sleeps an hour
a night. He says
his intercessory—
a needful and
unnecessary rite.

The Daemon Masque

Adam Bolivar

Over the hills and far away,
　　There was a sapphire isle,
Where never broke the light of day,
　　And lay a ruined pile,

The Castle Balladry 'twas called,
　　Where dwelt a gloomy duke,
For in this castle he was walled:
　　The Queen of Fae's rebuke.

But once upon a sevenyear,
　　He held a ghostly ball,
And all who were his kith and peer
　　Were bound by oath to call.

First came True Thomas gold of hair,
　　Who drowsed beneath a tree;
He saw the Queen so eldritch fair—
　　Her servant soon was he.

Mad Jack-a-Lee was next to come,
　　His boots with blood were red;
The balladress began to strum—
　　A troubadour, undead.

The King of Cats licked his grey paw,
    And hankered for a mouse,
Though all the night would hunger gnaw,
    For empty was the house.

The goblets held no crimson wine,
    And on the plates no meat,
Yet mortal guests ought not to whine,
    For phantoms do not eat.

Now Janet entered with Tam Lin,
    And Barbry Allen too;
The dancers reeled without, within,
    While o'er twa corbies crew.

A banshee keened a piercing wail,
    For three had struck the chimes;
The moon was hanging low and pale,
    And sang her final rhymes

The balladress who stilled her lyre,
    So quiet filled the hall,
And in the hearth there burned no fire;
    The darkness cast a pall.

The Devil came to reap his tithe,
    Due ev'ry sevenyear;
He took his payment with a scythe—
    A reckoning to fear.

For ballads were the Devil's cost,
    Which nevermore were sung,
To mortal memory then lost,
    Their words on no one's tongue.

And so the daemon masque was done,
    The ballads all had fled,
The King of Cats now all alone,
    In shadows left to tread.

A Word

Geoffrey Reiter

"The stream of Time, irresistible, ever moving, carries off and bears away all things that come to birth and plunges them into utter darkness . . . Nevertheless, the science of History is a great bulwark against this stream of Time; in a way it checks this irresistible flood, it holds in a tight grasp whatever it can seize floating on the surface and will not allow it to slip away into the depths of Oblivion."

—Anna Komnene, *The Alexiad* (translated by E. R. A. Sewter)

You feel it first, before you hear or see:
The sea o'erwhelming placid deltas, and
When Rahab's gullet spews her chaos free
Into the open channels, then the sand
And salt assault the tranquil stream and strand
Of land. I feel the fall of pressures in my gut
Of Time's remorseless current as I stand,
Await the plunge, to crush me like a nut
In some great hand, and hope feels futile. But
My words are mine, my one offense against
The brutal tide that fills the sky, for what
Else might I spit back at the beast? My tensed
Tongue lashing toward the serpent-shrouded day,
I cast my voice into the void and pray.

Moonlit Waters

Ashley Dioses

In winter twilight's darkened wake,
The shadows stretch across the lake.
The stars above, in gold and lime,
Will gleam until the end of time.

A faerie trail entwines with woods
Of pine and oak, where winter should
Caress her claws along your spine—
And yet you come toward water's line.

Defeated, like those here before,
The water lures you to its shore.
The noises in the icy air
Abruptly quiet their despair.

A silver mist awaits ahead
Where beckons it with other dead.
The towering firs and cedars reach
The sky where prowling owls screech.

Through silver mists the lake resides.
Its shimmering surface soon provides
A sanctuary from life's breath;
The moonlit waters grant you death.

Manurog

Manuel Arenas

Manurog lives in a bog, subsisting mainly on frogs
Sitting on half-sunken rocks, he draws a sprig 'twixt his locks.
Snagging on a shaggy knot, he halts to air a bon mot.
"How I wish I had a brush, groom my tousled mane to lush.
I once had a spiny comb, fashioned from a fallen gnome,
I'm so rough, it was brittle, crumbling to pieces little.
So, this tree branch must make do, till I make something from you!"

Black-Winged Battle Cry

Carl E. Reed

> The creativity and pathology of the human mind are, after all, two
> sides of the same medal coined in the evolutionary mint. The first
> is responsible for the splendour of our cathedrals, the second for
> the gargoyles that decorate them to remind us that the world is
> full of monsters, devils, and succubi.
>
> —Arthur Koestler

They carved my form from gray basaltic rock
cinder-burst into Triassic skies
when thunder lizards ruled afore the shock
from Chicxulub asteroid caused all to die.
Shapen by mammal hands into grotesque
winged form of fangs & razored claws,
I perch upon cathedral Romanesque
fell waterspout upon high buttressed wall.
At night I cleave from stone & soar in flight
hunting the hardened criminals who prowl
dark streets 'round Notre Dame; with righteous might
I descend on scurrying vermin with a growl
& battering shock of powerful black wings;
ripping flesh to get at viscera—soul sings!

Classic Reprints

The Deserted House

Alfred, Lord Tennyson

Life and Thought have gone away
    Side by side,
    Leaving door and windows wide:
Careless tenants they!

    All within is dark as night;
    In the windows is no light;
    And no murmur at the door,
    So frequent on its hinge before.

Close the door, the shutters close,
    Or thro' the windows we shall see
    The nakedness and vacancy
Of the dark deserted house.

Come away: no more of mirth
    Is here or merry-making sound.
The house was builded of the earth,
    And shall fall again to ground.

Come away: for Life and Thought
    Here no longer dwell;
    But in a city glorious—
A great and distant city—have brought
    A mansion incorruptible.
Would they could have staid with us!

[First published in Tennyson's *Poems, Chiefly Lyrical* (1830).]

The Vampire: 1914

Conrad Aiken

She rose among us where we lay.
She wept, we put our work away.
She chilled our laughter, stilled our play;
And spread a silence there.
And darkness shot across the sky,
And once, and twice, we heard her cry;
And saw her lift white hands on high
And toss her troubled hair.

What shape was this who came to us,
With basilisk eyes so ominous,
With mouth so sweet, so poisonous,
And tortured hands so pale?
We saw her wavering to and fro,
Through dark and wind we saw her go;
Yet what her name was did not know;
And felt our spirits fail.

We tried to turn away; but still
Above we heard her sorrow thrill;
And those that slept, they dreamed of ill
And dreadful things:
Of skies grown red with rending flames
And shuddering hills that cracked their frames;
Of twilights foul with wings;

And skeletons dancing to a tune;
And cries of children stifled soon;
And over all a blood-red moon
A dull and nightmare size.
They woke, and sought to go their ways,
Yet everywhere they met her gaze,
Her fixed and burning eyes.

Who are you now,—we cried to her—
Spirit so strange, so sinister?
We felt dead winds above us stir;
And in the darkness heard
A voice fall, singing, cloying sweet,
Heavily dropping, though that heat,
Heavy as honeyed pulses beat,
Slow word by anguished word.

And through the night strange music went
With voice and cry so darkly blent
We could not fathom what they meant;
Save only that they seemed
To thin the blood along our veins,
Foretelling vile, delirious pains,
And clouds divulging blood-red rains
Upon a hill undreamed.

And this we heard: "Who dies for me,
He shall possess me secretly,
My terrible beauty he shall see,
And slake my body's flame.
But who denies me cursed shall be,
And slain, and buried loathsomely,
And slimed upon with shame."

And darkness fell. And like a sea
Of stumbling deaths we followed, we
Who dared not stay behind.
There all night long beneath a cloud
We rose and fell, we struck and bowed,
We were the ploughman and the ploughed,
Our eyes were red and blind.

And some, they said, had touched her side,
Before she fled us there;
And some had taken her to bride;
And some lain down for her and died;
Who had not touched her hair,
Ran to and fro and cursed and cried
And sought her everywhere.

"Her eyes have feasted on the dead,
And small and shapely is her head,

And dark and small her mouth," they said,
"And beautiful to kiss;
  Her mouth is sinister and red
  As blood in moonlight is."

Then poets forgot their jeweled words
And cut the sky with glittering swords;
And innocent souls turned carrion birds
  To perch upon the dead.
Sweet daisy fields were drenched with death,
The air became a charnel breath,
Pale stones were splashed with red.

Green leaves were dappled bright with blood
And fruit trees murdered in the bud;
  And when at length the dawn
Came green as twilight from the east,
And all that heaving horror ceased,
Silent was every bird and beast,
  And that dark voice was gone.

No word was there, no song, no bell,
No furious tongue that dream to tell;
Only the dead, who rose and fell
  Above the wounded men;
And whisperings and wails of pain

Blown slowly from the wounded grain,
Blown slowly from the smoking plain;
And silence fallen again.

Until at dusk, from God knows where,
Beneath dark birds that filled the air,
Like one who did not hear or care,
Under a blood-red cloud,
An aged ploughman came alone
And drove his share through flesh and bone,
And turned them under to mould and stone;
All night long he ploughed.

[First published in the *New Republic* (9 April 1924).]

Reviews

Two Contemporaries, One Classic

S. T. Joshi

ASHLEY DIOSES. *The Withering.* Foreword by John Shirley. Illustrations by
Mutartis Boswell. Salem, OR: Jackanapes Press, 2020. 135 pp. $15.99 tpb.
ANN K. SCHWADER. *Unquiet Stars.* Central Point, OR: Weird House,
2021. ix, 81 pp. $14.95. tpb.
WILLIAM BLAKE. *Proverbs of Hell and Related Selections.* Edited by Oliver
Sheppard. Dallas, TX: Ikonograph Press, 2021. 107 pp. $15.00 tpb.

I am not at all convinced that gender, sexual orientation, or other such
factors play any significant role in the manner in which literature is
written. Critics who attempt to make distinctions between, say, male and
female writers all too often lapse into superficial and essentialist
arguments as to how gender affects their work—maintaining, for
example, that women writers are more empathetic or more adept at
portraying emotion. Oh? Are empathy and emotion lacking in male
writers? Are women writers incapable of depicting courage or
aggressiveness, two traits more commonly associated with men? In our
little field, it would seem that such distinctions are even more irrelevant.
The element of weirdness is not gender-specific; for every Edgar Allan
Poe there is a Mary Shelley.

That said, the enhanced literary opportunities now afforded to
female, gay, transgender, and other formerly disfavored groups is to be
enthusiastically welcomed; but such opportunities would defeat their
own purpose if the resulting work were not of intrinsic merit. Quality
remains the unassailable criterion of a literary work. And so, in assessing

the oeuvre of two living poets who happen to be female, I am happy to report that they are being considered here not because they are women, but because their poems are eminently worth reading.

Ashley Dioses's *The Withering* is her second poetry collection, following *Diary of a Sorceress* (2017). What this new collection displays above all else is the vitality that relatively conventional weird motifs can retain when manipulated by a skilled hand. Death, for example, is perhaps the oldest theme in literature as a whole, and yet Dioses in "Life Decayed" can infuse (pardon the pun) new life into it: "The icy hands that steal / The life-force out of you / Have now upheld their deal; / You join the Reaper's queue." Another age-old trope, the vampire, is rendered fresh and vivid in "Tears of Eternity," where the bloodsucker is pensively regretful of his (or her?) unholy need. The black widow spider who devours her mate is made the focus of "Cobwebs."

Numerous poems tell of the undead or of revenants—as in "Like a Fixed Star," where a queen is murdered by an unfaithful lover but is resurrected by a djinn and now seeks vengeance. In "All Hallows' Awakening," a corpse is revived by necromancers—but he (or she?) then exacts vengeance upon them: "At once, I fell into a sleep; / The agony is dire and deep. / My heart and soul are sparrow-black / With ice invading every crack."

In the lengthiest section of the book, "Night Cries," we find poems that appear to tread the borderline between supernatural and psychological terror. "Whispers" speaks of those whispers that "scream and shriek inside your weary head." Is this a metaphor for psychosis? This certainly seems to be the case in "Created," where the "eternal darkness" that haunts all our minds is the focus: "I am all things gone wrong in your sad life; / All the insanity that infiltrated. / Stabbed in your back, I'm the betraying knife. / Yes, I am everything that you created." The title poem of this section is a superb blend of horror and poignancy; it deserves to be quoted in full:

Upon this lonesome midnight hour
I pray the moon will wane in power.
I hear, when the pale moon is peaking,
The agony of lost souls shrieking.

It does not matter how they die,
You always hear their sad night cries.
None understand their lasting pain,
Yet they will always cry in vain.

"A Is for Axe Murderer" is a tour de force in which every letter of the alphabet signifies something relating to horror, death, blood, and so on. My favorite: "S is for the blissful screams / Pried from vilest lips."

In this book, Dioses reveals an admirable mastery of numerous different verse forms, from the quatrain to rhyming couplets to poems with internal rhymes (à la Poe's "The Raven" or Coleridge's *Rime of the Ancient Mariner*). If any biographical fact is of relevance in the analysis of this book, it is that, as Dioses (b. 1990) announces in her afterword, many of the poems in this book were written between 2002 and 2007—in other words, between her twelfth and seventeenth years. A more striking exhibition of youthful precocity would be difficult to find in contemporary literature: I am confident that no reader who has not read that afterword could possibly detect any difference in fundamental quality between the products of Dioses's early years and work of more recent vintage. This book—liberally and vibrantly illustrated by Mutartis Boswell—confirms Dioses's standing as one of the preeminent weird poets of our day.

Ann K. Schwader (b. 1960) published her first book of poetry in the year of Ashley Dioses's birth, and she has gone on to become one of the most stellar voices in contemporary weird verse. *Unquiet Stars* contains a sheaf of memorable poetry whose overall thrust appears to be the evocation of the appalling and aeon-weighted antiquity of the earth, and perhaps of the entire cosmos, rendering our own tenancy of it a derisively fleeting and insignificant phenomenon. One of the earlier poems in the book, "Children of the Stone," emphasizes how human beings have not always been the masters of this planet. Several poems about Egypt underscore this basic theme, while "Temple of the Condor" (on Machu Picchu) and the strikingly innovative "The Vestals" (on the Vestal Virgins of Rome) have a similar import. "The Distant Deaths of Galaxies" is one of several science-fictional poems that express cosmicism more purely; but the motif is evoked poignantly in "The City in the Sands":

No hand of man raised up the nameless stones
That formed this place. No human thought concerned
Its guardians—for we are not alone,
& never have been through the eons flown
Since void-spawned terrors taught our world to grieve.

As befits a writer well aware of the long literary heritage of
weirdness—and of poetry in general—Schwader writes homages to several
predecessors by whom she has been inspired. "Corridors Enough" is a
nod to Emily Dickinson. Several poems use the work of H. P. Lovecraft
as a springboard, perhaps none more notable than the long poem "A
Wizard's Daughter," on Asenath Waite, the hapless offspring of
Ephraim Waite, who in "The Thing on the Doorstep" took over his
daughter's body as a way of prolonging his existence. An entire cycle of
poems, "Faces from the House of Pain," extrapolates upon themes in
H. G. Wells's *The Island of Dr. Moreau,* bringing out the numerous
plangent undercurrents—the pain of a new hybrid identity, the paradox
of being not fully human nor fully animal, the godlike arrogance of the
heartless scientist who subjected his creatures to increasingly bizarre
experimentation—implicit in that novel. Schwader concludes: "We found
them dead together, in the end, / creator & creation each unmade / in
one red moment."

We now come to the third book under consideration here. It seems
vaguely presumptuous to "review" a poet of the status of William Blake,
but this book does not actually contain much that can be traditionally
regarded as poetry. *Proverbs of Hell* is, in large part, a reprint of a section of
Blake's *Marriage of Heaven and Hell* (1794), presenting actual proverbs—
seventy-one of them—that echo, and in some sense parody, the proverbs
in the Bible. What these texts reveal is a hostility to organized religion,
specifically Christianity, that is bracing and occasionally amusing.

The proverbs themselves fall into a long line of gnomic utterances, at
times mundane and at other times utterly inscrutable, going back at least
to the Presocratic philosopher Heraclitus (535?–475? B.C.E.). Blake
himself appears to have been influenced to some degree by the Swedish
mystic Emanuel Swedenborg, although one section of this book
pungently criticizes him. It would be easy to portray Blake as an outright
atheist (along the lines of his contemporary Percy Bysshe Shelley) on the

strength of such aphorisms as "Men forgot that Deities reside in the human breast"; but a writer of his complexity cannot be so easily categorised. What do we make of this? "Jesus is the only God. But so am I and so are you."

Other proverbs reveal a shrewd worldly wisdom in contrast to the standard view of Blake as a pie-in-the-sky mystic: "Prisons are built with stones of Law, Brothels with bricks of Religion." The editor, Oliver Sheppard, helpfully provides in an appendix a set of aphorisms by Johann Kaspar Lavater that may also have influenced Blake; but he makes the unwise decision to include a series of his own aphorisms whose jejune inanity does not do him credit. Nevertheless, this book is well worth securing as an introduction to one facet of Blake's baffling and unsystematic worldview.

An Aesthetic of Grotesquerie

Leigh Blackmore

K. A. OPPERMAN. *The Laughter of Ghouls*. Illustrated by Dan V. Sauer. New York: Hippocampus Press, 2021. 174 pp. $15.00 tpb.

The appearance of a new volume of weird verse by K. A. Opperman is always to be welcomed. The author of *The Crimson Tome* (Hippocampus Press, 2016) and *Past the Glad and Sunlit Season: Poems for Hallowe'en* (Jackanapes Press, 2020) now presents a comprehensive assemblage of his work—upwards of fifty poems—published in a wide variety of magazines and anthologies between 2015 and 2019. Opperman's prolificity is indeed admirable in one so young, especially since the work is of uniformly high quality.

Is it possible Opperman's title was inspired by Robert E. Howard's line in his poem "Fragment" (in *Always Comes Evening*): "Ever at his back / he heard the lecherous laughter of the ghouls"? Or was it, perhaps, inspired by the title of Robert Bloch's short story "The Laughter of a Ghoul" (*Fantasy Fan*, December 1934)? More likely, Opperman conceived his title independently—great macabre minds think alike—and the first poem here lends the volume its title. His line: "I have heard it of midnights, the laughter of ghouls" sets the tone for this entire gathering of horrific verse.

The book is divided into five thematic sections: "Graveyards Forgotten," "Carpathian Spells," "Ghostly Sighs," "Songs of the Goat," and "Nightshade Flowers." Opperman's subject matter is largely his own, though here and there he tips his poetic top hat to the greats of the genre. "Daemonic Nathicana" is a riff on, or sequel to, Lovecraft's poem

"Nathicana"—a poem itself echoing the rhythms of some of Poe's work and (unusually for Lovecraft) focusing on the dark beauties of the woman depicted. An example of Opperman's originality within this pastiche is his use of such delicious rhymes as that of "iguana" with "Nathicana." "Cassilda Dons the Pallid Mask" effectively adds to the lore and legend of Robert W. Chambers's King in Yellow Mythos—a body of pastiche and tribute that now far outweighs the slender original output of Chambers himself in this Mythos.

The short section "Graveyards Forgotten" (six poems) serves to draw the reader into the realms of the ravening ghouls. In "Carpathian Spells" the focus is strictly Gothic, and Opperman's inspirations include Le Fanu ("Carmilla") and Sacher-Masoch ("The Black Czarina"). Poems in this section extol the dark allure of the bat, the werewolf, the black rose, the succubus, the harpy, and the vampire. But lest such themes be considered too hackneyed, we must mark the poet's words in his introduction: "I believe there are deep-rooted reasons why these themes have been explored and re-explored for centuries, and I have sought to revivify them. I have attempted to distill the most pure and perfect essence of these subjects, so that they may shine with renewed clarity in our modern age, freed from the obscuring fogs of antiquity." And while Opperman does not hesitate to use old-fashioned language in such verses as "Wilhelmina"—"levin," "clomb," etc.—his conceptions are so vividly realized and his ability so unwavering that he very largely achieves his aims.

In the section "Songs of the Goat" we find several poems inspired by paintings by such artists as Jules Joseph Lefebvre, John Collier, and Goya, several inspired by stories by author Richard Gavin, and paeans to pagan goddesses including Diana and Ashtoreth (the latter dedicated to David Park Barnitz, author of *The Book of Jade*). Others focus on witches, sabbats and the mythology of Walpurgisnacht.

The poems in "Ghostly Sighs" are pure spectral weirdness telling of femmes fatales, ghostly spirits, phantasms, and death. All are equally effective, whether short or long, and Opperman varies his rhyme-schemes with refreshing frequency.

In "Nightshade Flowers," the themes transition from poems dealing with the eternal figure of the femme fatale (several dedicated to the poet's partner) through verses suggestively fungoid in focus. Others, all fantastical, deal with waves and ships and gargoyles, and finally with funerals and requiems, bringing the reader full circle to the grave, where the volume began. This section contains what may be one of Opperman's most nihilistic verses, "Crimson Masquerade"—a grim view of human existence whose final sextet must be quoted:

> Chaos incarnate roams these gloomy halls,
> A vast and formless demon many-legged;
> Puppets of entropy, delusions dolls,
> The masquers form a monster that has plagued
> Humanity from since the dawn of time,
> His every moment but a jester's rhyme.

Dan Sauer, whose digitally composed collage illustrations for various volumes in modern horror now position him as the twenty-first-century Harry O. Morris or J. K. Potter, provides a wealth of amplifications of the poems, including sections motifs and illustrations to particular poems. His fine cover for this volume, in its shades of funereal scarlet and purple, is particularly noteworthy.

The Laughter of Ghouls, though strengthened by echoes of macabre poets from Baudelaire and Poe to moderns such as D. L. Myers and Adam Bolivar, is successful principally because of the purity of Opperman's own commitment to an aesthetic of grotesquerie and his concentrated visions of poetic nightmare.

Notes on Contributors

Manuel Arenas is a writer of verse and prose in the Gothic horror tradition. His work has appeared in *Spectral Realms* and *Penumbra* as well as in various genre anthologies, including (most recently) *Knock Knock: Wyrd Folks and Wives' Tales* from Frisson Comics. He currently resides in Phoenix, Arizona, where he pens his dark ditties sheltered behind heavy curtains, as he shuns the oppressive orb which glares down on him from the cloudless, dust-filled sky.

David Barker is coauthor of three books of Lovecraftian fiction with the late W. H. Pugmire: *The Revenant of Rebecca Pascal, In the Gulfs of Dream and Other Lovecraftian Tales*, and *Witches in Dreamland*. His collection of horror fiction, *Her Wan Embrace*, is due from Weird House in 2021, and his story "Who Maketh Fertile the Fields" appeared in *A Walk in a Darker Wood: An Anthology of Folk Horror* in 2020.

F. J. Bergmann edits poetry for *Mobius: The Journal of Social Change* and imagines tragedies on or near exoplanets. His work appears irregularly in *Analog, Asimov's, Polu Texni, Pulp Literature, Silver Blade*, and elsewhere. *A Catalogue of the Further Suns*, a collection of dystopian first-contact poems, won the 2017 Gold Line Press poetry chapbook contest and is available at fibitz.com.

Leigh Blackmore's horror fiction has appeared in over sixty magazines from *Avatar* to *Strange Detective Stories*. He has reviewed for journals including *Lovecraft Annual, Shoggoth, Skinned Alive*, and *Dead Reckonings*. His critical essays appear in volumes including Benjamin Szumskyj's *The Man Who Collected Psychos: Critical Essays on Robert Bloch*, Gary William Crawford's *Ramsey Campbell: Critical Essays on the Modern Master of Horror*, Danel Olson's *21st Century Gothic*, and elsewhere. New weird verse has appeared in *Penumbra* and other journals.

Adam Bolivar, a native of Boston now residing in Portland, Oregon, has published his weird fiction and poetry in the pages of *Nameless,* the *Lovecraft eZine, Spectral Realms,* and Chaosium's *Steampunk Cthulhu* and *Atomic Age Cthulhu* anthologies. His latest collection, *The Lay of Old Hex,* was published in 2017 by Hippocampus Press. *Ballads for the Witching Hour* is forthcoming.

Frank Coffman is a retired professor of English and Creative Writing. He has published speculative poetry and short fiction in a variety of magazines, anthologies, and collections. His three collections of poetry are: *The Coven's Hornbook and Other Poems* (2019), *Black Flames and Gleaming Shadows* (2020), and *Eclipse of the Moon* (2021). His collection of seven occult detective mysteries, *Three against the Dark,* will be released this year.

Scott J. Couturier is a poet and prose writer of the weird, liminal, and darkly fantastic. His work has appeared in numerous venues, including *The Audient Void, Eye to the Telescope, The Dark Corner Zine, Space and Time,* and *Weirdbook.* Currently he works as a copy and content editor for Mission Point Press, living an obscure reverie in the wilds of northern Michigan with his partner/live-in editor and two cats. His debut short story collection, *The Box,* is due out in 2021 from Silent Motorist Media.

Ashley Dioses is a writer of dark fantasy and horror poetry from Southern California. Her debut poetry collection, *Diary of a Sorceress,* was published by Hippocampus Press in 2017. Her second collection, of early works, *The Withering,* appeared from Jackanapes Press in 2020. Her poem "Cobwebs" is mentioned in Ellen Datlow's *Best Horror of the Year,* Volume Twelve. She was also a nominee for the 2019 Pushcart Prize. She is an active member in the HWA and a member of the SFPA.

Joshua Gage is an ornery curmudgeon from Cleveland. He is the author of five collections of poetry. His chapbook *Necromancy* is available on Locofo Chaps from Moria Press. He is a graduate of the Low Residency MFA Program in Creative Writing at Naropa University. He has a penchant for Pendleton shirts and any poem strong enough to yank the breath out of his lungs.

Wade German is the author of the poetry collections *Dreams from a Black Nebula* (Hippocampus Press), *The Ladies of the Everlasting Lichen and Other Relics* (Mount Abraxas Press), the verse drama *Children of Hypnos*, and two slim volumes of verse in Portuguese translation, *Incantations* and *Apparitions* (Raphus Press).

Maxwell I. Gold is a Rhysling Award–nominated author of weird fiction, writing short stories and prose poems that center upon his profane Cyber Gods Mythos. His work has appeared in numerous publications including *The Audient Void, Space and Time, Weirdbook,* and many others.

P. B. Grant hails from Scotland and currently lives in Nova Scotia, Canada. His poetry, essays, and articles have been widely published in a variety of books and journals.

Chad Hensley is a Bram Stoker Award–nominated author. His most recent book of poetry, *Embrace the Hideous Immaculate,* was published by Raw Dog Screaming Press. His nonfiction has appeared in the magazines *Rue Morgue, Juxtapoz, Terrorizer, Spin, Hustler,* and most recently *Weird Fiction Review* no. 11, featuring his in-depth article on Cadabra Records, which includes commentary from Thomas Ligotti and S. T. Joshi. Look for his poetry in *Weirdbook* nos. 43, 44, and 45 along with *Skelos* no. 4 and his fiction in *Weirdbook's* upcoming zombie themed annual.

Alicia Hilton is an author, law professor, arbitrator, actor, and former FBI Special Agent. Her work has appeared in Akashic Books, *Daily Science Fiction, Departure Mirror, DreamForge, Dreams & Nightmares, Litro, Modern Haiku, Neon, Sci Phi Journal, Space and Time, Spectral Realms, Vastarien, Year's Best Hardcore Horror* volumes 4, 5, and 6, and elsewhere.

S. T. Joshi is a widely published critic and editor. He has prepared editions of the collected poetry of H. P. Lovecraft, Clark Ashton Smith, Donald Wandrei, George Sterling, and H. L. Mencken. He is the editor of *Spectral Realms.*

Lori R. Lopez is a quirky author, illustrator, poet, and songwriter who likes to wear hats. Her Gothic-toned and generous poetry collection

Darkverse: The Shadow Hours was nominated for the 2018 Elgin Award, while individual poems have been nominated for Rhysling Awards. Stories and verse have appeared in numerous publications. Other titles include *The Dark Mister Snark, Leery Lane,* and *An Ill Wind Blows.*

Charles Lovecraft studies English at Macquarie University, Sydney. His main literary and life influences have been H. P. Lovecraft and macabre literature. More than 150 of his poems have been published. As publisher-editor he runs weird poetry imprint P'rea Press (www.preapress.com). He is working on a long Lovecraftian weird poem, *The Caller of Darkness,* and has edited thirty-four books.

Josh Maybrook is a poet, scholar, bibliophile, and proponent of traditional verse forms. Many of his poems engage with supernatural themes and have appeared in journals such as *Spectral Realms, Night to Dawn, Lovecraftiana,* and *Veil: Journal of Darker Musings.*

D. L. Myers is a dark poet from the Pacific Northwest. His work has appeared in *Spectral Realms, Eye to the Telescope, The Audient Void, Black Wings VI, The Rhysling Anthology, Test Patterns,* and *A Walk in a Darker Wood.* His first collection, *Oracles from the Black Pool,* was published by Hippocampus Press in 2019.

Ngo Binh Anh Khoa is a teacher of English in Ho Chi Minh City, Vietnam. In his free time, he enjoys daydreaming, reading, and occasionally writing poetry for personal entertainment. His speculative poems have appeared in NewMyths.com, *Heroic Fantasy Quarterly, The Audient Void,* and other venues.

K. A. Opperman is a poet with a predilection for the strange, the Gothic, and the grotesque, continuing the macabre and fantastical tradition of such luminaries as Poe, Clark Ashton Smith, and H. P. Lovecraft. He has published three poetry collections to date: *The Crimson Tome, Past the Glad and Sunlit Season,* and *The Laughter of Ghouls.*

Manuel Pérez-Campos's poetry has appeared previously in *Spectral Realms* and *Weird Fiction Review.* A collection of his poetry in the key of the weird is in progress; so is a collection of ground-breaking essays on H. P. Lovecraft. He lives in Bayamón, Puerto Rico.

Justin Permenter is a writer of poetry, short fiction, novels, and screenplays from Corinth, Texas. He holds a B.A. in Russian from Baylor University and a Master's of International Affairs from the Bush School of Government & Public Service at Texas A&M. Whenever he is not writing, he operates undercover as a college admissions counselor and recruiter. His work has been published in *Hypertext Review, Scarlet Leaf Review,* and at *365 tomorrows.*

Carl E. Reed is showroom manager for a window, siding, and door company just outside Chicago. Former jobs include U.S. marine, long-haul trucker, improvisational actor, cab driver, security guard, bus driver, door-to-door encyclopedia salesman, construction worker, and art show MC. His poetry has been published in the *Iconoclast* and *Spectral Realms;* short stories in *Black Gate* and *newWitch* magazines.

Geoffrey Reiter is Associate Professor and Coordinator of Literature at Lancaster Bible College. He is also an Associate Editor at the website Christ and Pop Culture, where he frequently writes about weird horror and dark fantasy. As a scholar of weird fiction, Reiter has published academic articles on such authors as Arthur Machen, Bram Stoker, Clark Ashton Smith, and William Peter Blatty. His creative work has previously appeared in *Spectral Realms,* with more to come in the upcoming volume of *Penumbra.*

Ann K. Schwader lives and writes in Colorado. Her newest collection, *Unquiet Stars,* is now out from Weird House Press. Two of her earlier collections, *Wild Hunt of the Stars* (Sam's Dot, 2010) and *Dark Energies* (P'rea Press, 2015), were Bram Stoker Award Finalists. In 2018, she received the Science Fiction & Fantasy Poetry Association's Grand Master award. She is also a two-time Rhysling Award winner.

Darrell Schweitzer has finally gotten his overdue third collection of poetry. *Dancing Before Azathoth* will be published soon by P'rea Press, with an introduction by S. T. Joshi. His other two poetry collections are *Groping toward the Light* (2002) and *Ghosts of Past and Future* (2010), both available from Wildside Press. His ambition is to be one day better known for these than for rhyming Cthulhu in a limerick. He is otherwise a short-story writer, novelist, essayist, anthologist, and a former editor of *Weird Tales.*

Claire Smith writes poetry about other worlds. Her work regularly appears in *Spectral Realms.* Most recently her poems have also featured in *Songs of Eretz, Corvid Queen, Illumen,* and *Sage Cigarettes.* She holds an M.A. in English from the Open University and is currently studying for a Ph.D. at the University of Gloucestershire. Claire lives in Gloucestershire with her husband and their very spoiled Tonkinese cat, Ishtar.

Oliver Smith is a visual artist and writer from Cheltenham, UK. His poetry has appeared in *Mirror Dance, Dreams & Nightmares, Rivet, Strange Horizons, Liminality,* and *Penumbric.* Oliver was awarded first place in the BSFS 2019 competition for his poem "Better Living through Witchcraft," and his poem "Lost Palace, Lighted Tracks" was nominated for the 2020 Pushcart Prize. In 2020 he was awarded a Ph.D. in Literary and Critical Studies.

Jay Sturner is a writer, poet, and naturalist from the Chicago suburbs. He is the author of several books of poetry and a collection of short stories. He has been nominated twice for the Rhysling Award, and in 2019 one of his poems was featured on a segment of NPR's *All Things Considered.* In addition to being a writer, Sturner is also a professional bird walk leader.

DJ Tyrer is the person behind Atlantean Publishing and has been published in *The Rhysling Anthology,* issues of *Cyäegha, The Horrorzine, Scifaikuest, Sirens Call, Star*Line, Tigershark,* and *The Yellow Zine.* The echapbook *One Vision* is available from Tigershark Publishing. *SuperTrump* and *A Wuhan Whodunnit* are available for download from Atlantean Publishing.

M. F. Webb's poetry has appeared in previous issues of *Spectral Realms* and her fiction has been published in *Latchkey Tales.* She resides in a Victorian seaport town not too far from Seattle with her husband and their five adult cats plus one pandemic kitten.

Abigail Wildes is a poet and author, a crafter, a seamstress, and an occultist. Her first book, *Tea with Death,* is in stores across the world and is a finalist for two awards. Besides being extremely busy with two creatures of chaos (a.k.a. children), Abigail has four books coming in 2021–22: *The Missed Carriage, Whoops-Y-Daisy Daisy, The Eco-Witch,* and the highly anticipated sequel to *Tea with Death, Let's Eat Cake.*

Steven Withrow's most recent verse collection is *The Bedlam Philharmonic.* His poems appear in *Spectral Realms, Asimov's Science Fiction,* and *Dreams & Nightmares.* His short poem "The Sun Ships," from a collection of the same title, was nominated for a 2016 Rhysling Award from the Science Fiction & Fantasy Poetry Association. He lives in Falmouth, Massachusetts.

Jordan Zuniga is an emerging Christian creative writer who actively writes and promotes on Instagram@cccreativewriter and on vocal.media as Jordan Zuniga. He is actively seeking new opportunities to share his work and is currently seeking representation from a literary agent for a high fantasy novel.

CPSIA information can be obtained
at www.ICGtesting.com
Printed in the USA
BVHW041345050921
615962BV00007B/109